Sp

Pre-Scho... for Childi... ...i.. Special Needs

Brenda Robson

CITY COLLEGE
LEARNING RESOURCE SERVICE
WITHDRAWN FROM STOCK

EAST BIRMINGHAM COLLEGE
Women's Academy
Learning Resource Centre

CASSELL

Cassell Educational Limited
Wellington House
125 Strand, London
WC2R 0BB

Copyright © Brenda Robson 1989

All rights reserved. No part of this publication may be
reproduced or transmitted in any form or by any means,
electronic or mechanical including photocopying, recording
or any information storage or retrieval system, without
prior permission in writing from the publishers.

First published 1989, Reprinted 1996

British Library Cataloguing in Publication Data

Robson, Brenda
    Pre-school provision for children with
    special needs.—(Special needs in ordinary
    schools)
    1. Great Britain. Special nursery education
    I. Title II. Series
    371.9'0941

ISBN: 0–304–31559–1

Phototypesetting by Activity Ltd., Salisbury, Wilts.
Printed and bound in Great Britain by
Redwood Books, Trowbridge, Wiltshire.

CLASS
371·9   A

ACC.
035699

Contents

EAST BIRMINGHAM COLLEGE
Women's Academy
Learning Resource Centre

Acknowledgements

The writing of this book has been made possible by the support of a number of people to whom I wish to express thanks.

The DES funded the research in which I was involved and some of which is reported here. This research was directed by Margaret M. Clark, who has provided immeasurable professional and personal guidance and encouragement during the past decade.

Peter Mittler is to be thanked for very useful editorial comments and Juliet Wight-Boycott for her patience and encouragement. On the domestic front, Lorna Miller provided invaluable practical help and my long-suffering husband, Michael, was always there to provide much needed love and understanding. Finally, I wish to express my love to my own three pre-schoolers, Gordon, Fergus and Calum, who have added many new dimensions to my understanding of young children and who have, in their own individual ways, contributed to this book.

To Jean and Bill Cunningham, my mother and father

Foreword: Towards education for all

AIMS

This series aims to support teachers as they respond to the challenge they face in meeting the needs of all children in their school, particularly those identified as having special educational needs.

Although there have been many useful publications in the field of special educational needs during the last decade, the distinguishing feature of the present series of volumes lies in their concern with specific areas of the curriculum in primary and secondary schools. We have tried to produce a series of conceptually coherent and professionally relevant books, each of which is concerned with ways in which children with varying levels of ability and motivation can be taught together. The books draw on the experience of practising teachers, teacher trainers and researchers and seek to provide practical guidelines on ways in which specific areas of the curriculum can be made more accessible to all children. The volumes provide many examples of curriculum adaptation, class-room activities, teacher–child interactions, as well as the mobilisation of resources inside and outside the school.

The series is organised largely in terms of age and subject groupings, but three 'overview' volumes have been prepared in order to provide an account of some major current issues and developments. Seamus Hegarty's *Meeting Special Needs in Ordinary Schools* gives an introduction to the field of special needs as a whole, whilst Sheila Wolfendale's *Primary Schools and Special Needs* and John Sayer's *Secondary Schools for All?* address issues more specifically concerned with primary and secondary schools respectively. We hope that curriculum specialists will find essential background and contextual material in these overview volumes.

In addition, a section of this series will be concerned with examples of obstacles to learning. All of these specific special needs can be seen on a continuum ranging from mild to severe, or from temporary and transient to long-standing or permanent. These include difficulties in learning or in adjustment and behaviour, as well as problems resulting largely from sensory or physical impairments or from difficulties of communication from whatever cause. We hope that teachers will consult the volumes in this section for guidance on working with children with specific difficulties.

The series aims to make a modest 'distance learning' contribution to meeting the needs of teachers working with the whole range of pupils with special educational needs by offering a set of resource materials relating to specific areas of the primary and secondary curriculum and by suggesting ways in which learning obstacles, whatever their origin, can be identified and addressed.

We hope that these materials will not only be used for private study but be subjected to critical scrutiny by school-based inservice groups sharing common curricular interests and by staff of institutions of higher education concerned with both special needs teaching and specific curriculum areas. The series has been planned to provide a resource for Local Education Authority (LEA) advisers, specialist teachers from all sectors of the education service, educational psychologists, and teacher working parties. We hope that the books will provide a stimulus for dialogue and serve as catalysts for improved practice.

It is our hope that parents will also be encouraged to read about new ideas in teaching children with special needs so that they can be in a better position to work in partnership with teachers on the basis of an informed and critical understanding of current difficulties and developments. The goal of 'Education for All' can only be reached if we succeed in developing a working partnership between teachers, pupils, parents, and the community at large.

ELEMENTS OF A WHOLE-SCHOOL APPROACH

Meeting special educational needs in ordinary schools is much more than a process of opening school doors to admit children previously placed in special schools. It involves a radical re-examination of what all schools have to offer all children. Our efforts will be judged in the long term by our success with children who are already in ordinary schools but whose needs are not being met, for whatever reason.

The additional challenge of achieving full educational as well as social integration for children now in special schools needs to be seen in the wider context of a major reappraisal of what ordinary schools have to offer the pupils already in them. The debate about integration of handicapped and disabled children in ordinary schools should not be allowed to overshadow the movement for curriculum reform in the schools themselves. If successful, this could promote the fuller integration of the children already in the schools.

If this is the aim of current policy, as it is of this series of unit texts, we have to begin by examining ways in which schools and school policies can themselves be a major element in children's difficulties.

Can schools cause special needs?

Traditionally, we have looked for causes of learning difficulty in the child. Children have been subjected to tests and investigations by doctors, psychologists and teachers with the aim of pinpointing the nature of the problem and in the hope that this might lead to specific programmes of teaching and intervention. We less frequently ask ourselves whether what and how we teach and the way in which we organise and manage our schools could themselves be a major cause of children's difficulties.

The shift of emphasis towards a whole-school policy is sometimes described in terms of a move away from the deficit or medical model of special education towards a more environmental or ecological model. Clearly, we are concerned here with an interaction between the two. No one would deny that the origins of some learning difficulties do lie in the child. But even where a clear cause can be established — for example, a child with severe brain damage, or one with a serious sensory or motor disorder — it would be simplistic to attribute all the child's learning difficulties to the basic impairment alone.

The ecological model starts from the position that the growth and development of children can be understood only in relation to the nature of their interactions with the various environments which impinge on them and with which they are constantly interacting. These environments include the home and each individual member of the immediate and extended family. Equally important are other children in the neighbourhood and at school, as well as people with whom the child comes into casual or closer contact. We also need to consider the local and wider community and its various institutions — not least, the powerful influence of television, which for some children represents more hours of information intake than is provided by teachers during eleven years of compulsory education. The ecological model thus describes a gradually widening series of concentric circles, each of which provides a powerful series of influences and possibilities for interaction — and therefore learning.

Schools and schooling are only one of many environmental influences affecting the development and learning of children. A great deal has been learned from other environments before the child enters school and much more will be learned after the child leaves full-time education. Schools represent a relatively powerful series of environments, not all concerned with formal learning. During the hours spent in school, it is hard to estimate the extent to which the number and nature of the interactions experienced by any one child are directly concerned with formal teaching and learning. Social interactions with other children also need to be considered.

Questions concerned with access to the curriculum lie at the heart of any whole-school policy. What factors limit the access of certain children to the curriculum? What modifications are necessary to ensure fuller curriculum access? Are there areas of the curriculum from which some children are excluded? Is this because they are thought 'unlikely to be able to benefit'? And even if they are physically present, are there particular lessons or activities which are inaccessible because textbooks or worksheets demand a level of literacy and comprehension which effectively prevent access? Are there tasks in which children partly or wholly fail to understand the language which the teacher is using? Are some teaching styles inappropriate for individual children?

Is it possible that some learning difficulties arise from the ways in which schools are organised and managed? For example, what messages are we conveying when we separate some children from others? How does the language we use to describe certain children reflect our own values and assumptions? How do schools transmit value judgements about children who succeed and those who do not? In the days when there was talk of comprehensive schools being 'grammar schools for all', what hope was there for children who were experiencing significant learning difficulties? And even today, what messages are we transmitting to children and their peers when we exclude them from participation in some school activities? How many children with special needs will be entered for the new General Certificate of Secondary Education (GCSE) examinations? How many have taken or will take part in Technical and Vocational Education Initiative (TVEI) schemes?

The argument here is not that all children should have access to all aspects of the curriculum. Rather it is a plea for the individualisation of learning opportunities for all children. This requires a broad curriculum with a rich choice of learning opportunities designed to suit the very wide range of individual needs.

Curriculum reform

The last decade has seen an increasingly interventionist approach by Her Majesty's Inspectors of Education (HMI), by officials of the Department of Education and Science (DES) and by individual Secretaries of State. The 'Great Debate', allegedly beginning in 1976, led to a flood of curriculum guidelines from the centre. The garden is secret no longer. Whilst Britain is far from the centrally imposed curriculum found in some other countries, government is increasingly insisting that schools must reflect certain key areas of experience for all pupils, and in particular those concerned with the world of work (*sic*), with science and technology, and with economic awareness. These priorities are also reflected in the prescriptions for teacher education laid down with an increasing degree of firmness from the centre.

There are indications that a major reappraisal of curriculum content and access is already under way and seems to be well supported by teachers. Perhaps the best known and most recent examples can be found in the series of Inner London Education Authority (ILEA) reports concerned with secondary, primary and special education, known as the Hargreaves, Thomas and Fish Reports (ILEA, 1984, 1985a, 1985b). In particular, the Hargreaves Report envisaged a radical reform of the secondary curriculum, based to some extent on his book *Challenge for the Comprehensive School* (Hargreaves, 1982). This envisages a major shift of emphasis from the 'cognitive–academic' curriculum of many secondary schools towards one emphasising more personal involvement by pupils in selecting their own patterns of study from a wider range of choice. If the proposals in these reports were to be even partially implemented, pupils with special needs would stand to benefit from such a wholesale review of the curriculum of the school as a whole.

Pupils with special needs also stand to benefit from other developments in mainstream education. These include new approaches to records of achievement, particularly 'profiling' and a greater emphasis on criterion-referenced assessment. Some caution has already been expressed about the extent to which the new GCSE examinations will reach less able children previously excluded from the Certificate of Secondary Education. Similar caution is justified in relation to the TVEI and the Certificate of Pre-Vocational Education (CPVE). And what about the new training initiatives for school leavers and the 14–19 age group in general? Certainly, the pronouncements of the Manpower Services Commission (MSC) emphasise a policy of provision for all, and have made specific arrangements for young people with special needs, including those with disabilities. In the last analysis, society and its institutions will be judged by their success in preparing the majority of young people to make an effective and valued contribution to the community as a whole.

A CLIMATE OF CHANGE

Despite the very real and sometimes overwhelming difficulties faced by schools and teachers as a result of underfunding and professional unrest, there are encouraging signs of change and reform which, if successful, could have a significant impact not only on children with special needs but on all children. Some of these are briefly mentioned below.

The campaign for equal opportunities

First, we are more aware of the need to confront issues concerned with civil rights and equal opportunities. All professionals concerned with human services are being asked to examine their own attitudes and practices and to question the extent to which these might unwittingly or even deliberately discriminate unfairly against some sections of the population.

We are more conscious than ever of the need to take positive steps to promote the full access of girls and women not only to full educational opportunities but also to the whole range of community resources and services, including employment, leisure, housing, social security and the right to property. We have a similar concern for members of ethnic and religious groups who have been and still are victims of discrimination and restricted opportunities for participation in society and its institutions. It is no accident that the title of the Swann Report on children from ethnic minorities was *Education for All* (Committee of Inquiry, 1985). This too is the theme of the present series and the underlying aim of the movement to meet the whole range of special needs in ordinary schools.

The equal opportunities movement has not itself always fully accepted people with disabilities and special needs. At national level, there is no legislation specifically concerned with discrimination against people with disabilities, though this does exist in some other countries. The Equal Opportunities Commission does not concern itself with disability issues. On the other hand, an increasing number of local authorities and large corporations claim to be 'Equal Opportunities Employers', specifically mentioning disability alongside gender, ethnicity and sexual orientation. Furthermore, the 1986 Disabled Persons Act, arising from a private member's Bill and now on the statute book, seeks to carry forward for adults some of the more positive features of the 1981 Education Act — for example, it provides for the rights of all people with disabilities to take part or be represented in discussion and decision-making concerning services provided for them.

These developments, however, have been largely concerned with children or adults with disabilities, rather than with children already in ordinary schools. Powerful voluntary organisations such as MENCAP (the Royal Society for Mentally Handicapped Children and Adults) and the Spastics Society have helped to raise political and public awareness of the needs of children with disabilities and have fought hard and on the whole successfully to secure better services for them and for their families. Similarly, organisations of adults with disabilities, such as the British Council of Organisations for Disabled People, are pressing hard for better quality, integrated education, given their own personal experiences of segregated provision.

Special needs and social disadvantage

Even these developments have largely bypassed two of the largest groups now in special schools: those with moderate learning difficulties and those with emotional and behavioural difficulties. There are no powerful pressure groups to speak for them, for the same reason that no pressure groups speak for the needs of children with special needs already in ordinary schools. Many of these children come from families which do not readily form themselves into associations and pressure groups. Many of their parents are unemployed, on low incomes or dependent on social security; many live in overcrowded conditions in poor quality housing or have long-standing health problems. Some members of these families have themselves experienced school failure and rejection as children.

Problems of poverty and disadvantage are common in families of children with special needs already in ordinary schools. Low achievement and social disadvantage are clearly associated, though it is important not to assume that there is a simple relation between them. Although most children from socially disadvantaged backgrounds have not been identified as low achieving, there is still a high correlation between social-class membership and educational achievement, with middle-class children distancing themselves increasingly in educational achievements and perhaps also socially from children from working-class backgrounds — another form of segregation within what purports to be the mainstream.

The probability of socially disadvantaged children being identified as having special needs is very much greater than in other children. An early estimate suggested that it was more than seven times as high, when social disadvantage was defined by the presence of all three of the following indices: overcrowding (more than 1.5 persons per room), low income (supplementary benefit or free school meals) and adverse family circumstances (coming from a single-parent home or a home with more than five children) (Wedge and Prosser, 1973). Since this study was published, the number of families coming into these categories has greatly increased as a result of deteriorating economic conditions and changing social circumstances.

In this wider sense, the problem of special needs is largely a problem of social disadvantage and poverty. Children with special needs are therefore doubly vulnerable to underestimation of their abilities: first, because of their family and social backgrounds, and second, because of their low achievements. A recent large-scale study of special needs provision in junior schools suggests that while teachers' attitudes to low-achieving children are broadly positive, they are pessimistic about the ability of such children to derive much benefit from increased special needs provision (Croll and Moses, 1985).

Partnership with parents

The Croll and Moses survey of junior school practice confirms that teachers still tend to attribute many children's difficulties to adverse home circumstances. How many times have we heard comments along the lines of 'What can you expect from a child from that kind of family?' Is this not a form of stereotyping at least as damaging as racist and sexist attitudes?

Partnership with parents of socially disadvantaged children thus presents a very different challenge from that portrayed in the many reports of successful practice in some special schools. Nevertheless, the challenge can be and is being met. Paul Widlake's recent books (1984, 1985) give the lie to the oft-expressed view that some parents are 'not interested in their child's education'. Widlake documents project after project in which teachers and parents have worked well together. Many of these projects have involved teachers visiting homes rather than parents attending school meetings. There is also now ample research to show that children whose parents listen to them reading at home tend to read better and to enjoy reading more than other children (Topping and Wolfendale, 1985; see also Sheila Wolfendale's *Primary Schools and Special Needs*, in the present series).

Support in the classroom

If teachers in ordinary schools are to identify and meet the whole range of special needs, including those of children currently in special schools, they are entitled to support. Above all, this must come from the headteacher and from the senior staff of the school; from any special needs specialists or teams already in the school; from members of the new advisory and support services, as well as from educational psychologists, social workers and any health professionals who may be involved.

This support can take many forms. In the past, support meant removing the child for considerable periods of time into the care of remedial teachers either within the school or coming from outside. Withdrawal now tends to be discouraged, partly because it is thought to be another form of segregation within the ordinary school, and therefore in danger of isolating and stigmatising children, and partly because it deprives children of access to lessons and activities available to other children. In a major survey of special needs provision in middle and secondary schools, Clunies-Ross and Wimhurst (1983) showed that children with special needs were most often withdrawn from science and modern languages in order to find the time to give them extra help with literacy.

Many schools and LEAs are exploring ways in which both teachers and children can be supported without withdrawing children from ordinary classes. For example, special needs teachers increasingly are working alongside their colleagues in ordinary classrooms, not just with a small group of children with special needs but also with all children. Others are working as consultants to their colleagues in discussing the level of difficulty demanded of children following a particular course or specific lesson. An account of recent developments in consultancy is given in Hanko (1985), with particular reference to children with difficulties of behaviour or adjustment.

Although traditional remedial education is undergoing radical reform, major problems remain. Implementation of new approaches is uneven both between and within LEAs. Many schools still have a remedial department or are visited by peripatetic remedial teachers who withdraw children for extra tuition in reading with little time for consultation with school staff. Withdrawal is still the preferred mode of providing extra help in primary schools, as suggested in surveys of current practice (Clunies-Ross and Wimhurst, 1983; Hodgson, Clunies-Ross and Hegarty, 1984; Croll and Moses, 1985).

Nevertheless, an increasing number of schools now see withdrawal as only one of a widening range of options, only to be used where the child's individually assessed needs suggest that this is indeed the most appropriate form of provision. Other alternatives are now being considered. The overall aim of most of these involves the development of a working partnership between the ordinary class teacher and members of teams with particular responsibility for meeting special needs. This partnership can take a variety of forms, depending on particular circumstances and individual preferences. Much depends on the sheer credibility of special needs teachers, their perceived capacity to offer support and advice and, where necessary, direct, practical help.

We can think of the presence of the specialist teacher as being on a continuum of visibility. A 'high-profile' specialist may sit alongside a pupil with special needs, providing direct assistance and support in participating in activities being followed by the rest of the class. A 'low-profile' specialist may join with a colleague in what is in effect a team-teaching situation, perhaps spending a little more time with individuals or groups with special needs. An even lower profile is provided by teachers who may not set foot in the classroom at all but who may spend considerable periods of time in discussion with colleagues on ways in which the curriculum can be made more accessible to all children in the class, including the least able. Such discussions may involve an examination of textbooks and other reading assignments for readability, conceptual difficulty and relevance of content, as well as issues concerned with the presentation of the material, language modes and complexity used to explain what is required, and the use of different approaches to teacher–pupil dialogue.

IMPLICATIONS FOR TEACHER TRAINING

Issues of training are raised by the authors of the three overview works in this series but permeate all the volumes concerned with specific areas of the curriculum or specific areas of special needs.

The scale and complexity of changes taking place in the field of special needs and the necessary transformation of the teacher-training curriculum imply an agenda for teacher training that is nothing less than retraining and supporting every teacher in the country in working with pupils with special needs.

Although teacher training represented one of the three major priorities identified by the Warnock Committee, the resources devoted to this priority have been meagre, despite a strong commitment to training from teachers, LEAs, staff of higher education, HMI and the DES itself. Nevertheless, some positive developments can be noted (for more detailed accounts of developments in teacher education see Sayer and Jones, 1985 and Robson, Sebba, Mittler and Davies, 1988).

Initial training

At the initial training level, we now find an insistence that all teachers in training must be exposed to a compulsory component concerned with meeting special needs in the ordinary school. The Council for the Accreditation of Teacher Education (CATE) and HMI seem set to enforce these criteria; institutions that do not meet them will not be accredited for teacher training.

Although this policy is welcome from a special needs perspective, many questions remain. Where will the staff to teach these courses come from? What happened to the Warnock recommendations for each teacher-training institution to have a small team of staff specifically concerned with this area? Even when a team exists, they can succeed in 'permeating' a special needs element into initial teacher training only to the extent that they influence all their fellow specialist tutors to widen their teaching perspectives to include children with special needs.

Special needs departments in higher education face similar problems to those confronting special needs teams in secondary schools. They need to gain access to and influence the work of the whole institution. They also need to avoid the situation where the very existence of an active special needs department results in colleagues regarding special needs as someone else's responsibility, not theirs.

Despite these problems, the outlook in the long term is favourable. More and more teachers in training are at least receiving an introduction to special needs; are being encouraged to seek out information on special needs policy and practice in the schools in which they are doing their teaching practice, and are being introduced to a variety of approaches to meeting their needs. Teaching materials are being prepared specifically for initial teacher-training students. Teacher trainers have also been greatly encouraged by the obvious interest and commitment of students to children with special needs; optional and elective courses on this subject have always been over-subscribed.

Inservice courses for designated teachers

Since 1983, the government has funded a series of one-term full-time courses in polytechnics and universities to provide intensive training for designated teachers with specific responsibility for pupils with special needs in ordinary schools (see *Meeting Special Needs in Ordinary Schools* by Seamus Hegarty in this series for information on research on evaluation of their effectiveness). These courses are innovative in a number of respects. They bring LEA and higher-education staff together in a productive working partnership. The seconded teacher, headteacher, LEA adviser and higher-education tutor enter into a commitment to train and support the teachers in becoming change agents in their own schools. Students spend two days a week in their own schools initiating and implementing change. All teachers with designated responsibilities for pupils with special needs have the right to be considered for these one-term courses, which are now a national priority area for which central funding is available. However, not all teachers can gain access to these courses as the institutions are geographically very unevenly distributed.

Other inservice courses

The future of inservice education for teachers (INSET) in education in general and special needs in particular is in a state of transition. Since April 1987, the government has abolished the central pooling arrangements which previously funded courses and has replaced these by a system in which LEAs are required to identify their training requirements and to submit these to the DES for funding. LEAs are being asked to negotiate training needs with each school as part of a policy of staff development and appraisal. Special needs is one of nineteen national priority areas that will receive 70 per cent funding from the DES, as is training for further education (FE) staff with special needs responsibilities.

These new arrangements, known as Grant Related Inservice Training (GRIST), will change the face of inservice training for all teachers but time is needed to assess their impact on training opportunities and teacher effectiveness (see Mittler, 1986, for an interim account of the implications of the proposed changes). In the meantime, there is serious concern about the future of secondments for courses longer than one term. Additional staffing will also be needed in higher education to respond to the wider range of demand.

An increasing number of 'teaching packages' have become available for teachers working with pupils with special needs. Some (though not all) of these are well designed and evaluated. Most of them are school-based and can be used by small groups of teachers working under the supervision of a trained tutor.

The best known of these is the Special Needs Action Programme (SNAP) originally developed for Coventry primary schools (Muncey and Ainscow, 1982) but now being adapted for secondary schools. This is based on a form of pyramid training in which co-ordinators from each school are trained to train colleagues in their own school or sometimes in a consortium of local schools. Evaluation by a National Foundation for Educational Research (NFER) research team suggests that SNAP is potentially an effective approach to school-based inservice training, providing that strong management support is guaranteed by the headteacher and by senior LEA staff (see Hegarty, *Meeting Special Needs in Ordinary Schools*, this series, for a brief summary).

Does training work?

Many readers of this series of books are likely to have recent experience of training courses. How many of them led to changes in classroom practice? How often have teachers been frustrated by their inability to introduce and implement change in their schools on returning from a course? How many heads actively support their staff in becoming change agents? How many teachers returning from advanced one-year courses have experienced 'the re-entry phenomenon'? At worst, this is quite simply being ignored: neither the LEA adviser, nor the head nor any one else asks about special interests and skills developed on the course and how these could be most effectively put to good use in the school. Instead, the returning member of staff is put through various re-initiation rituals ('Enjoyed your holiday?'), or is given responsibilities bearing no relation to interests developed on the course. Not infrequently, colleagues with less experience and fewer qualifications are promoted over their heads during their absence.

At a time of major initiatives in training, it may seem churlish to raise questions about the effectiveness of staff training. It is necessary to do so because training resources are limited and because the morale and motivation of the teaching force depend on satisfaction with what is offered — indeed, on opportunities to negotiate what is available with course providers. Blind faith in training for training's sake soon leads to disillusionment and frustration.

For the last three years, a team of researchers at Manchester University and Huddersfield Polytechnic have been involved in a DES funded project which aimed to assess the impact of a range of inservice courses on teachers working with pupils with special educational needs (see Robson, Sebba, Mittler and Davies, 1988, for a full account and Sebba and Robson, 1987, for a briefer interim report). A variety of courses was evaluated; some were held for one evening a week for a term; others were one-week full time; some were award-bearing, others were not. The former included the North-West regional diploma in special needs, the first example of a course developed in total partnership between a university and a polytechnic which allows students to take modules from either institution and also gives credit recognition to specific Open University and LEA courses. The research also evaluated the effectiveness of an already published and disseminated course on behavioural methods of teaching — the EDY course (Farrell, 1985).

Whether or not the readers of these books are or will be experiencing a training course, or whether their training consists only of the reading of one or more of the books in this series, it may be useful to conclude by highlighting a number of challenges facing teachers and teacher trainers in the coming decades.

1. We are all out of date in relation to the challenges that we face in our work.

2. Training in isolation achieves very little. Training must be seen as part of a wider programme of change and development of the institution as a whole.
3. Each LEA, each school and each agency needs to develop a strategic approach to staff development, involving detailed identification of training and development needs with the staff as a whole and with each individual member of staff.
4. There must be a commitment by management to enable the staff member to try to implement ideas and methods learned on the course.
5. This implies a corresponding commitment by the training institutions to prepare the student to become an agent of change.
6. There is more to training than attending courses. Much can be learned simply by visiting other schools, seeing teachers and other professionals at work in different settings and exchanging ideas and experiences. Many valuable training experiences can be arranged within a single school or agency, or by a group of teachers from different schools meeting regularly to carry out an agreed task.
7. There is now no shortage of books, periodicals, videos and audio-visual aids concerned with the field of special needs. Every school should therefore have a small staff library which can be used as a resource by staff and parents. We hope that the present series of unit texts will make a useful contribution to such a library.

The publishers and I would like to thank the many people — too numerous to mention — who have helped to create this series. In particular we would like to thank the Associate Editors, James Hogg, Peter Pumfrey, Tessa Roberts and Colin Robson, for their active advice and guidance; the Honorary Advisory Board, Neville Bennett, Marion Blythman, George Cooke, John Fish, Ken Jones, Sylvia Phillips, Klaus Wedell and Phillip Williams, for their comments and suggestions; and the teachers, teacher trainers and special needs advisers who took part in our information surveys.

Professor Peter Mittler
University of Manchester

REFERENCES

Clunies-Ross, L. and Wimhurst, S. (1983) *The Right Balance: Provision for Slow Learners in Secondary Schools*. Windsor: NFER/Nelson.

Committee of Inquiry (1985) *Education for All*. London: HMSO (The Swann Report).

Croll, P. and Moses, D. (1985) *One in Five: The Assessment and Incidence of Special Educational Needs*. London: Routledge & Kegan Paul.

Farrell, P. (ed.) (1985) *EDY: Its Impact on Staff Training in Mental Handicap*. Manchester: Manchester University Press.

Hanko, G. (1985) *Special Needs in Ordinary Classrooms: An Approach to Teacher Support and Pupil Care in Primary and Secondary Schools*. Oxford: Blackwell.

Hargreaves, D. (1982) *Challenge for the Comprehensive School*. London: Routledge & Kegan Paul.

Hodgson, A., Clunies-Ross, L. and Hegarty, S. (1984) *Learning Together*. Windsor: NFER/Nelson.

Inner London Education Authority (1984) *Improving Secondary Education*. London: ILEA (The Hargreaves Report).

Inner London Education Authority (1985a) *Improving Primary Schools*. London: ILEA (The Thomas Report).

Inner London Education Authority (1985b) *Equal Opportunities for All?* London: ILEA (The Fish Report).

Mittler, P. (1986) The new look in inservice training, *British Journal of Special Education*, **13**, 50–51.

Muncey, J. and Ainscow, M. (1982) Launching SNAP in Coventry. *Special Education: Forward Trends*, **10**, 3–5.

Robson, C., Sebba, J., Mittler, P. and Davies, G. (1988) *Inservice Training and Special Needs: Running Short School-Focused Courses*. Manchester: Manchester University Press.

Sayer, J. and Jones, N. (eds) (1985) *Teacher Training and Special Educational Needs*. Beckenham: Croom Helm.

Sebba, J. and Robson, C. (1987) The development of short, school-focused INSET courses in special educational needs. *Research Papers in Education* **2**, 1–29.

Topping, K. and Wolfendale, S. (eds) (1985) *Parental Involvement in Children's Reading*. Beckenham: Croom Helm.

Wedge, P. and Prosser, H. (1973) *Born to Fail?* London: National Children's Bureau.

Widlake, P. (1984) *How to Reach the Hard to Teach*. Milton Keynes: Open University Press.

Widlake, P. (1985) *Reducing Educational Disadvantage*. London: Routledge & Kegan Paul.

Preface

This series of books reflects the changes which are taking place within society as a whole, and within education specifically, in relation to the provisions which are made for young people with special educational needs. Current theory and practice are moving away from segregated special education towards the integration of greater numbers of children with special needs into ordinary educational facilities.

This is the only book in the series that focuses on the pre-school years. Pre-school education certainly encompasses a very short space of time within a child's overall educational experience. Local authorities are not required to provide pre-school education. Consequently, attendance is not compulsory. The value of pre-school education has been strongly attacked in recent years and its very existence has, at times, been under threat. Paradoxically, few would argue with the view that the pre-school child has a vast capacity for learning. Physical growth and language development are readily observed but equally important foundations are laid in the areas of cognitive development, social skills, moral attitudes and emotional stability. This book will show how pre-school education of a high quality can contribute significantly to all aspects of the learning process and maximise a child's potential in numerous ways. The first section of the book outlines the development of pre-school education in this country. The historical separation of day care and pre-school education will be highlighted to provide a context for the divergent provision which exists today and the attempts to remedy this situation. There is a strong case for an integrated pre-school service that emphasises both care and education. Indeed, the distinction between these two aspects of pre-school provision is, in reality, meaningless when considering the overall growth and development of young children.

Clearly, the whole concept of the integration of pre-school children with special needs would be in jeopardy without a firm commitment to the development of an integrated pre-school service providing care and education. It is only as a result of a high standard of physical care that many children will be in a position to take advantage of the educational experiences offered in the nursery.

After establishing the value of pre-school provision and arguing for the development of an integrated service, the book will focus on practical aspects of integrating children with special needs. It would be useful at this point, however, to consider why we should want to integrate pre-school children with special needs into ordinary nurseries. I would begin with the very basic argument that it is morally wrong to remove a child from a normal environment at the age of only 2 or 3 years, unless that child has profound difficulties which would severely limit the benefits to be gained from ordinary nursery attendance. The proportion of such children is very small indeed. The nursery environment is traditionally informal, with an emphasis on free play and individual choice. The curriculum should be flexible. There are no formal examinations to place constraints on teaching and learning, and the whole ethos of the nursery should make parental involvement a reality in the widest sense. It follows, therefore, that ordinary nursery education should be able to accommodate children with a wide range of special needs. It only requires that central government and local education authorities be fully supportive, not only by expressing positive attitudes towards integration but by allocating necessary resources in terms of staffing levels, staff training, professional support and equipment. The following chapters will make it clear that integration does not just happen because children with special needs are placed in ordinary nurseries. Integration is not a cheap alternative to segregated provision.

The concept of pre-school education as laying foundations for future development and experience has important implications for the integration of children with special needs. Carefully planned integration of such children into ordinary nursery schools and classes can only enhance the likelihood of successful integration at infant and primary level and beyond. Children with special needs learn to interact with their peers and have opportunities to learn from other children. At the same time, their peers learn about special needs. Social integration in the nursery school may ease transition into primary school where the child is already an accepted member of the community. Ongoing assessment and observation of the child in the nursery will provide the infant teacher with useful and relevant records outlining strengths and weaknesses, which will also contribute to successful integration. Experience suggests that a child with special needs who has been integrated into an ordinary nursery is much more likely to move into an ordinary infant class, and to remain there, than a child who has attended a segregated special nursery from an early age.

So far, discussion has centred on those young children who have identifiable special needs but nurseries have additional important roles to play within the wider nature of special needs. The Warnock Committee suggested that some 20 per cent of children will have special educational needs at some time in their school careers. It may be that nursery education can help to prevent or minimise some of these learning difficulties by providing children with a stimulating and relevant curriculum at a crucial stage in their development. Improved record-keeping and assessment procedures will lead to the earlier identification of special needs and hence earlier intervention to minimise long-term effects.

—1——————————————————————

Integration of pre-school children with special needs: not one step but two

In an extensive series of books looking at special needs in ordinary schools, this is the only book focusing specifically on the pre-school child. The majority of the books in the series examine aspects of the integration of children with special needs into ordinary primary and secondary schools. Within primary education there is certainly no uniformity of provision and wide variations will be found across schools in terms of classroom organisation, curriculum, assessment, staff training and so on. It is generally accepted, however, that primary education is well-established, is beneficial for our children and is here to stay. Similarly, authors considering secondary education can be fairly confident that the reader supports the concept of secondary education even though the educational content and role of assessment, among other things, are widely debated.

In contrast, the very relevance and value of pre-school education have been the subject of vigorous debate throughout this century, and the debate has gained momentum during the past two decades. Successive governments have been ambivalent about the desirability of nursery growth as reflected in legislation which, while permitting and possibly advocating nursery expansion, has not made such growth the statutory duty of local education authorities. Consequently, there is wide variation throughout the country in the extent and nature of pre-school provision. These points will be expanded later in this chapter and it will be argued in the next chapter that research has not assisted policy makers and legislators by producing conflicting and often confusing findings and conclusions.

Before consideration of the question of integrating pre-school children with special needs it is necessary to examine the nature of the provision into which they are to be integrated and to justify the very existence of that provision. Integration in this book will have two quite distinct meanings, referring not only to the inclusion of children with special needs in ordinary nursery education but also to the need to integrate the various forms of pre-school provision into a unified service for the under-fives. The current status of educational pre-school provision and social services pre-school provision, and the recent moves towards combined nursery centres, can best be understood within a historical context. The development of pre-school provision in Britain will be discussed in some detail, following the pattern of growth throughout this century and the recent changes in government policy which threaten this expansion. The contribution of research towards our understanding of the pre-school child and the value of nursery attendance will be considered together with some relevant issues and areas of controversy. First, however, clarification of the term 'pre-school' is necessary.

DEFINING 'PRE-SCHOOL'

The term 'pre-school' has been over-used in recent years. It has been used extensively to describe the child who has not yet started compulsory education but, as Woodhead (1979) points out, this is not particularly helpful in widely disseminated research and literature, since the pre-school child might be under 7 years of age in Scandinavia, under 5 in Britain and under 6 in most other countries. Indeed, a child of 4 years 1 month might already be in infant school under one English education authority while a child of over 5 years of age in the neighbouring authority might still be a pre-schooler.

To consider pre-school as a noun is equally bewildering and unhelpful since there is no such entity as 'the pre-school'. Northam (1983) distinguishes numerous forms of pre-school provision including:

1. Nursery schools and classes.
2. Combined centres.
3. Local authority day nurseries.
4. Workplace day nurseries.
5. Private day nurseries.
6. Private nursery schools.
7. Childminders.
8. Pre-school playgroups.

Even within these categories there is considerable diversity of organisation. Northam claims, for example, that there are 16 ways of organising playgroups.

Pre-school will be defined for present purposes as referring to children who have not yet reached the statutory age of beginning infant or primary school. There is wide regional variation in the exact age at which children enter school, as will be discussed later, but it is likely that all children, under normal circumstances, will be in school by the age of 5½ years. Since this book forms part of a series of books concerned with special needs in ordinary educational establishments, the focus will be on nursery schools and classes, and combined centres where there is significant 'educational' input. Reference will often be made to day nurseries and playgroups, which cater for large numbers of pre-school children, and many of the arguments and proposals put forward will be relevant to these forms of provision.

A CENTURY OF DEVELOPMENT: 1840–1940

The first pre-school facilities appeared in Europe in the mid-nineteenth century, followed by remarkably rapid expansion. The first creche opened in Paris in 1844, receiving government recognition some 20 years later. Germany followed by opening *Bewahranstalten* and in Belgium *Jardins des Enfants* came into being. Froebel's first kindergarten opened in 1837 in Austria and by 1872 staff training had been established, administered by the Ministry of Education. By the turn of the century 50 per cent of 2–5-year-olds in Belgium, 25 per cent in France and 10 per cent in Germany attended some form of pre-school provision (van der Eyken, 1977).

This movement in Europe was resisted in Britain, where it was claimed that fewer women were in employment and so there was limited demand. Robert Owen, the New Lanark reformer, was the only pioneer on the British scene in the nineteenth century. In 1816 he opened the Institution for the Formation of Character to cater for the under-fives of the women employed in his factories and mills in New Lanark in Scotland, demonstrating an advanced philosophy and social consciousness which was at odds with the rest of British society.

The fact that Britain took no initiative in the early development of pre-school provision did not mean that pre-school children remained at home with their families. Parents could, if they wished, send their under-fives to elementary schools and this is probably the main reason for failure to provide nursery schools and classes. By the turn of the century some 43 per cent of 3–5-year-olds attended elementary schools. There being no separate facilities for them, they were compelled to mix with older children and sit at desks all day. When this practice was condemned by a Board of Education report in 1905, the government recommended that it should cease but gave local education authorities discretion to provide alternative facilities. The Education Act 1908 officially established free nursery education by giving LEAs the power to provide separate nursery classes in elementary schools. The government, therefore, gave LEAs discretionary powers but did not compel them to provide nursery education or allocate funds to enable them to do so. This policy of discretion rather than compulsion has been attached repeatedly to government legislation and has not helped to stimulate growth of pre-school provision.

The immediate effect of the Education Act 1908 was actually a decline in numbers of pre-school children being catered for (from 43 per cent in educational provision in 1900 to 13 per cent in 1926) due to the closing of elementary school doors and the lack of alternatives. By 1928 there were only 26 nursery schools in Britain.

Lack of government response to the needs of pre-school children stimulated the pioneering work of enlightened individuals who were motivated to improve the health and general well-being of children living in appalling social circumstances. Emphasis was on social welfare but there was a growing recognition of the educational value of nursery attendance. Ferri *et al.* (1981) note the interesting fact that many early nursery schools, such as that run by Rachel and Margaret McMillan in Deptford, were open for long hours in areas of high female employment and so, in effect, provided day care and educational input under one roof.

The Maternal and Child Welfare Act 1918, however, clearly established the administrative division between day care and education by giving responsibility for day nurseries to the Ministry of Health. The legacy of this legislation and the practical repercussions have led to the 'muddle and irrationality' (Tizard, J., 1975) of present day pre-school provision and attempts are still being made to reconcile the two services.

There was very little expansion in educational pre-school provision and day care between the wars. A Board of Education pamphlet (1936) entitled *Nursery Schools and Nursery Classes* sums up society's attitudes at this time in its opening sentence: 'Most people in this country are agreed that the proper place for children under five years old is the home'. The developmental needs of the child seemed secondary to political, economic and social factors and the pamphlet described the under-fives 'problem' as being due to 'modern housing conditions, the growth of traffic and all kinds of pressing social, industrial and financial considerations'. Open-air nursery schools were described as being primarily concerned with physical and medical nurture. The benefits of nursery education were, therefore, stressed as encompassing physical prowess ('they walk and run with unusual freedom and grace') and good behaviour. It was acknowledged that language skills might be enhanced since nursery children were said to be more articulate on entering school than non-attenders at nursery, but the quality of nursery children's speech was 'disappointing' due to the fact that they were left to play on their own for long periods and were too deeply engrossed in construction work!

1940 TO THE PRESENT DAY

The Second World War saw renewed government commitment to nursery education and a massive rise in day care provision. This rise in day nursery places was, however, short-lived. During the war, the Ministry of Health instigated a rapid increase in the availability of day nursery places to allow women to enter the labour force. The end of the war signalled an equally rapid dismantling of this provision. It was assumed that married women would return to the home. Indeed, it was seen as highly desirable that they should do so, a view strongly supported by Bowlby (1951). In 1946 grants to local authorities for day nurseries ceased. Day nursery numbers dropped from a peak in 1944 of 71,806 children to 21,530 children in 1964 (van der Eyken, 1977).

There has been little change since then in day nursery capacity but major changes have taken place in their clientele. They were no longer catering mainly for ordinary children of working parents but rather for children who had social and emotional problems as a result of unsatisfactory home conditions. This pattern was exacerbated in 1971 when local health authority departments transferred responsibility for day nurseries to the new social services departments. The effect of this policy, as summed up by Ferri *et al.* (1981), has been to 'concentrate a highly selective, disadvantaged population of children, often with diverse and acute needs, in a form of provision which has traditionally seen its role as confined to the promotion of physical welfare.'

Unfortunately the ethos of the day nursery and the training of staff did not change in line with the changing roles and demands to be met. Care continued to be emphasised and education ignored. The government did not seem to recognise or did not acknowledge the need for drastic re-appraisal of aims and objectives within day care provision. For example, a Scottish Education Department report, as recently as 1971, totally under-emphasised the problems faced by day nurseries by stating that they 'provide care, in cases of domestic difficulty, for young children or even babies whose parents cannot care for them during working hours' (Scottish Education Department, 1971).

Recent trends in nursery education have also been fraught with setbacks and ambiguities. The Education Act 1944 gave local education authorities powers to provide nursery schools and classes. Once again, however, there was no obligation to do so and the hoped-for expansion of nursery provision did not come to fruition. Indeed, faced with a shortage of teachers and a rising birth rate, a DES circular pronounced in 1960 that the sections of the Education Act 1944 relating to pre-school provision had not been implemented and that they would not be in the immediate future. The minimal expansion of nursery provision in the 1960s and early 1970s was, therefore, financed from special funds and not by direct government support. In 1964 there was a slight relaxation to allow for new building but new nursery places had to be allocated primarily to mothers who could teach (Kent and Kent, 1970). The Plowden Report (Department of Education and Science, 1967) led the way for some additional investment in nursery education in areas of greatest need, designated educational priority areas.

In 1972 the government took the unprecedented step of firmly pledging that, within 10 years, there should be free nursery education available for the 3–5-year-old children of all parents who desired that their children attend such provision. Unfortunately, economic factors once again intervened and this highly ambitious proposal was not carried through. By 1980 it was clear that local authorities could not, or would not, meet the recommendation to provide nursery education at this level. Manchester had the highest availability of nursery places, sending 50 per cent of eligible children to pre-school, but many authorities provided for less than 10 per cent, Gloucestershire had abolished all nursery education and Oxfordshire was about to follow suit (Passmore, 1980). The Education Act 1980 removed the statutory duty on all local education authorities to provide nursery education.

COMBINED NURSERY CENTRES

The divergent developmental paths of pre-school education and day care have led to a situation which is confusing for parents and clearly not in the best interests of children or staff. The need for reform is highlighted when considering the integration of young children with special needs into ordinary pre-school units. These children may have considerable requirements in terms of physical care and medical supervision but they also share with ordinary children the need for cognitive stimulation and a planned educational environment. A major new initiative in recent years has been the move towards a more child-centred approach, combining day care and education in one nursery centre. Some local authorities have taken steps in this direction by enabling the employment of teachers in day nurseries. More radical experiments have attempted to design new centres with joint education department and social services management. Because educational provision and day care developed in very different ways, this new concept is not straightforward in its implementation. Ferri *et al.* (1981) investigated several combined nursery centres and could not come up with a blueprint for the ideal unit since they were very varied. They highlighted some of the problems undermining successful development of integrated provision:

> The lack of effective co-operation between local authority departments, the perpetuation of different categories of place *within* combined centres, anomalies in staff working conditions and problems of staff and relationships – all these issues have their roots not in the *concept* of integrated provision, but in the somewhat entrenched attitudes and behaviour of the various policy-makers, administrators and practitioners.
>
> (p. 198)

Strathclyde Region in Scotland is attempting to set up an integrated pre-five service which will combine all forms of pre-school provision (Strathclyde Regional Council, 1985). Changes in administration and staffing have proved to be particularly difficult to instigate and it will be many years before the goals of the pre-five service are realised, but other local authorities will undoubtedly learn much from the experiences of the Strathclyde initiative.

The concept of combined nursery centres has, therefore, a long way to go before a truly integrated pre-school service can be provided. The problems can be overcome since combined centres are a logical step forward and will make a valuable and indeed necessary contribution to the integration of children with special needs, which, as will be argued throughout this book, calls for a more flexible and child-centred approach than is available within the diverse forms of traditional pre-school provision.

No specific mention has yet been made of the pre-school playgroup movement which began in the 1960s and which has been well documented elsewhere (e.g. Crowe, 1973). Playgroups provide valuable pre-school experience for large numbers of children but, for many reasons related to staffing, accommodation and the aims and objectives of playgroup provision, many would find it difficult to provide for children with special needs. Although many playgroups do not cater for children with special needs, some find that they must offer places to such children because of a lack of alternative provision in the area. The Pre-school Playgroup Association in Wales began a county referral scheme in Clwyd in 1983 and this has been extended throughout the country. Salaried co-ordinators are responsible for making arrangements for children with special needs to attend playgroups, for providing ongoing support to families and playgroup leaders and for linking with other agencies.

Although this series is concerned specifically with educational provision, playgroup leaders may find that the issues raised and suggestions made in this book are of interest and relevant to the handling of some of the children in their care.

NUMBERS OF CHILDREN ATTENDING PRE-SCHOOL PROVISION

Statistical records are collected separately for England, Scotland, Wales and Ireland and for several reasons it is very difficult to obtain a clear picture of the national pattern of pre-school attendance. Statistical returns may be made at different times of the academic year. It is often impossible to determine the numbers of 4-year-olds in nursery provision since they are not considered separately from those 4-year-olds already in reception classes. The Scottish Education Department uses the term 'nursery school' to refer to all pre-school education provision whereas the Department of Education and Science differentiates between nursery school and nursery class, although occasionally using 'nursery class' to refer to both types.

Bearing in mind these difficulties in interpreting regional figures, statistics suggest that in 1985 approximately 676,000 children attended nursery schools and classes in the United Kingdom, accounting for approximately 43 per cent of the estimated population of 3- and 4-year-olds. There has, therefore, been an increase in provision since 1975, when just over a quarter of 3- and 4-year-olds were receiving education. Part of this increase is due to a reduction in full-time places and steady increase in part-time places since 1980 and to earlier entry of 4-year-olds to school in some areas, but there is still an overall increase in the number of nursery places.

In 1985, 476,000 children attended maintained and registered playgroups and 59,000 children were to be found in maintained and registered day care provision (Central Statistical Office, 1987).

CONTRIBUTION OF RESEARCH

If the statistics are accurate, then over one million under-fives attend nursery schools and classes, day nurseries and playgroups in

Great Britain. Although this does not fully meet the demand for places, it nevertheless represents a considerable investment of resources in educating and caring for the pre-school child. Yet surprisingly little is known about the effects of pre-school experience, either in the short-term or in the long-term. The growth of pre-school provision has generally been based not on theories of child development or on research findings but, as we have seen, was determined more by economic, political and social factors.

This is not to say that researchers have ignored the pre-school child in the nursery. There is an abundance of literature devoted to pre-school education covering an enormous range of issues and behaviours. Studies have been aimed at understanding teacher behaviour in the nursery (e.g. Fagot, 1973; Tizard *et al.*, 1976a, b, c; Hamilton and Gordon, 1978) and the relative role of nursery nurses (e.g. Gipps, 1982a, b). Others have investigated the role of parents in the nursery (Donachy, 1976, 1979, 1987; Tizard *et al.*, 1981). We have information on the effects of space in the nursery (Smith and Connolly, 1980), assessment of pre-school children (Bate *et al.*, 1981), record keeping (Lomax, 1977), play patterns (Tizard *et al.*, 1976a, b, c), social behaviour (McGrew, 1972a, b) and even eating patterns at mealtimes (Baker *et al.*, 1983). Social class, sex differences, birth order, intelligence, personality and language have all received attention. The list of topics is endless and undoubtedly research such as this adds to our knowledge of the behaviour of children and adults in nurseries. But by concentrating on very specific behaviours or single aspects of the unit's organisation, such small scale studies do not throw light on the overall impact of pre-school education and the factors which contribute most to long-term effects.

An empirical evaluation of the effects of nursery education, however, cannot possibly control all the variables necessary in order to make valid generalisations. Even if the research worker concentrates on one pre-school unit, there will be numerous difficulties to overcome. As with any longitudinal study, children will be lost from the sample before completion of data collection. Voluntary attendance at nursery increases the likelihood of intermittent attendance by some children. Some will go on to the local designated primary school where follow-up study can be carried out. But with parental choice of school now in operation, some children may transfer to any of half a dozen schools in the vicinity, making it impossible to interpret the findings of any follow-up study. If evaluation of one nursery unit is difficult to carry out, then any generalisations about the relative effectiveness of different types of pre-school is an even more awesome task.

Bearing in mind the dangers of over-generalising from the findings of a limited research project, it is of some concern that bold and possibly unjustified statements can make considerable impact in the media. For example, Bain and Barnett (1981) studied 12 children in one day nursery in Ealing. They claimed that the children became more aggressive as a result of day nursery attendance and less able to cope with school. The consequent headline in the *Times Educational Supplement* read 'Day nurseries damage children' (Makins, 1981) and considerable consternation ensued.

Oxford Pre-School Research Project

This project, directed by J. Bruner between 1975 and 1978, was probably the most extensive study of its kind in recent years, involving pre-school educational provision, day nurseries, play-groups, childminders and the role of parents. The research was published as a series of six books, the first being an overview and discussion by Bruner (1980) and the others presenting details of the various studies which made up the research project.

Bruner summarises and interprets the findings of each of the five studies and it is only after reading these studies that two reservations become apparent. Firstly, Bruner did not directly oversee and plan the entire research. Each area was planned by a separate working party and the studies frequently evolved and changed direction as a result of discussions between the research workers and practitioners. This is not only a hazardous procedure within a research project but it also meant that five quite separate studies were carried out with little overall direction and supervision and, therefore, opportunities for generalisation and comparisons across provision were lost.

Secondly, Bruner presents findings without reference to difficulties encountered during the studies which might limit generalisability of the results. Some of these reservations were mentioned by the research workers in their books. Readers who do not go beyond Bruner's book to read the five others cannot, therefore, make their own judgements regarding the 'validity' of some of Bruner's interpretations.

Three of the studies are particularly relevant in this respect. Sylva *et al.* (1980) carried out direct structured observations of children in a sample of nursery schools and classes and playgroups. The sample of playgroups, however, was biased and untypical of playgroups generally and so comparisons with nursery schools and classes must be tentative. Garland and White (1980) observed children in nine day nurseries and their method of observing and recording introduced considerable subjectivity into their data. They spent more time observing in units that they felt were better and they did not pre-select children for study but rather followed those children who were felt to be doing interesting things. From the report by Wood *et al.* (1980) it would seem that this study found the most difficulty in terms of successful collaboration between research workers and practitioners, the latter having considerable say in the direction of the study. Nursery staff were recorded interacting with their children. Staff operated their own tape recorders, recording at times of their own choice, which suggests that interactions may not have been entirely typical and natural.

None of the above research reservations, most of which are noted by the research workers, were identified by Bruner. Much of the practical work carried out during the Oxford Pre-School Research Project was innovative and imaginative, undoubtedly producing findings which will be replicated elsewhere, but generalisations and comparisons between types of provision must be considered in conjunction with research difficulties and possible areas of bias and ambiguity.

Present uncertainty

Research which produces findings along the lines of 'day nurseries damage children' mentioned previously, must create a certain amount of insecurity and lack of confidence in politicians, practitioners, professional support services and parents. This insecurity was heightened by the publication of a research report by Tizard and Hughes (1984) which claimed that its main objective was 'to describe the ways in which young children learn from their mothers at home' (p. 1) but which went on to present very strong criticisms of the role and usefulness of nursery schools. The study involved the recording of girls' (no boys were included) interactions at home with their mothers and in nursery schools. Flaws in the design and methodology of this study make generalisations invalid, but the implications of the reported findings are of more concern here. Tizard and Hughes state that:

> ... many politicians and professionals believe that nursery school stimulates growth and language development .... There is very little British research evidence to substantiate these claims. Certainly this study suggests that children's intellectual and language needs are much more likely to be satisfied at home than at school.
>
> (p. 256)

Elsewhere the authors state that:

> The richness, depth and variety which characterised the home conversations was sadly missing (in nursery school). So too was the sense of intellectual struggle, and of the real attempts to communicate being made on both sides.
>
> (p. 9)

The authors concede that 'some parents will be worried by our findings' but they are placated by the knowledge that 'the children were certainly happy at school, for much of the time absorbed in play' and that nursery schools can offer some experiences not available at home, namely the opportunity to get on with other children, to get used to separation from their families, to relate to strange adults and to run around. Politicians and administrators will not be satisfied with such platitudes. They do not sanction the investment of millions of pounds in nursery education so that children can get used to strange adults and run around happily. If these findings were correct, then the closure of nursery schools and classes as they exist would be justified.

Pre-school education is, therefore, in a state of flux. The government has diverted considerable funding and commissioned a great deal of research under the Nursery Education Research Programme but critical evaluation of that evidence has not been forthcoming. It is not surprising, therefore, that Sir Keith Joseph, then Education Secretary, announced in February 1985 that the DES had commissioned a critical evaluation of all research into the education of under-fives undertaken over recent years (Clark, 1988). Sir Keith Joseph explained the need for such a study by saying that:

> There is now a very substantial amount of research findings in this field and there is a need, which I believe is shared by academics, practitioners, administrators and elected members of LEAs, to take stock and assess the validity and significance of the results of this research.
>
> (DES Press Notice, 27 February 1985)

Clark (1988) provides a thorough examination of pre-school research in the United Kingdom during the past two decades. She found very wide variations in the type and quality of provision available to children in different parts of the country.

> Whether or not a particular child attends, and which provision, whether there is any choice, whether attendance is full or part-time, depends on the exact area in which the child lives, the child's precise date of birth and the parents' knowledge of available provision.
>
> (p. 276)

Clark concluded that there is a need for greater resources, further training of staff and co-ordination of services for under-fives. Research priorities were identified which included:

1. Studies cf continuity of children's experiences between 3 and 7 or 8 years of age.
2. The development of literacy and numeracy in young children.
3. The particular problems of children for whom English is a second language.
4. The needs of children in rural areas.
5. Surveys of pre-service and inservice courses available nationally for teachers and other staff working with young children.
6. Evaluation of the extent and quality of educational and other provision for children under 5 in order to assess the extent to which this is meeting current needs.

It is true to say that research has provided little conclusive evidence regarding the long-term effects of nursery education. Indeed, in the 1960s and 1970s the highly publicised and well-documented Head Start pre-school programmes in the USA suggested that any gains made by children in pre-school education were not maintained in the following years. Curtis (1986) points out, however, that re-assessment of some of the original data and follow-up studies indicate the presence of persistent pre-school educational benefits (Lazar, 1978; Weikart *et al.*, 1978; Dye, 1984). I have argued that many studies in pre-school education have focused very narrowly on specific behaviours and larger scale studies have often failed to overcome methodological difficulties, making generalisation of findings invalid. As a result, researchers have failed to provide clear directives and positive guidelines for policy makers in the field of pre-school education but, on the other hand, no research project has conclusively found that pre-school education is a pointless exercise.

PRE-SCHOOL CHILDREN WITH SPECIAL NEEDS

The development of pre-school provision has been described in some detail because the present controversies and uncertainty can only be understood within a historical context. The development of special pre-school provision requires relatively little discussion for two reasons. Firstly, a historical outline of special education is provided elsewhere in this series (e.g. Hegarty, 1987). Secondly, throughout the past century government commitment to pre-school provision and to special education has been ambiguous and frequently half-hearted. The handicapped pre-school child has been particularly neglected. Early legislation dealing with the education of handicapped children was mainly concerned with those over the age of 5 or 7 years. Handicapped pre-schoolers will have been found in charitable private nurseries, special nursery classes, ordinary nurseries and playgroups (where staff have been agreeable to their admission) and at home.

The Education Act 1981

The Warnock Report (Department of Education and Science, 1978) is the first document to emphasise provision for the handicapped *pre-school* child and indeed considers this as one of three areas of immediate priority. The Education Act 1981 gave legislative force to some of the recommendations of the Warnock Report. Again, the details of this Act are fully discussed in Hegarty (1987) and only those aspects of relevance to pre-school children will be mentioned here.

The 1981 Act contained some innovatory ideas within the field of special education which amended the legal requirements as laid down by the Education Act 1944, this being the previous major piece of legislation governing special education. It brought about a new concept of special educational need following the recommendations of the Warnock Report. LEAs were given particular duties in the provision of special education, which was to take place as far as possible within ordinary schools and classes (although section 2.3 of the Act gave LEAs considerable scope to opt for segregated special school placement, as will be discussed below). Procedures for the assessment of special educational need were clearly defined and the rights of parents to participate in this assessment and to appeal were also established.

The Act stressed the need for early intervention and for the first time LEAs were empowered to assess and provide educational services for children with special needs below the age of 2 years, if their parents wished this. For children over the age of 2 years and under the age of 5, the LEA must carry out formal assessment if parents make a reasonable request and this is likely to be followed by a statement of the child's special educational needs and recommendations for educational assistance and/or placement. Again, parents have the right to refuse to send their child under the age of 5 years to nursery but, as Davis (1984) points out, parents are much influenced by the opinion of professionals regarding the need for provision. The onus is firmly placed on parents to seek educational assistance for children with special needs in the pre-school years, although section 10 of the Act makes it the duty of area and district health authorities to inform parents and the LEA of the possibility that a pre-school child may have special needs.

At first sight, the 1981 Act seems to pave the way for extensive integration of pre-school children with special needs into ordinary nursery schools and classes. There are, however, several reasons why this has not occurred, and need not occur, on a wide scale. Firstly, as mentioned above, section 2.3 of the Act stipulates the necessary conditions for integration to occur and states that educating the child in an ordinary school must be compatible with the special provision which is required by the child, the provision of efficient education for the other children in the class or school and the efficient use of resources. The term 'efficient' is not defined. These conditions are expressed in such a way that LEAs could readily argue that one or more cannot be met. They may even argue that it is not efficient use of resources to leave an unoccupied place in a special school if a child could fill it (Swann, 1985).

Secondly, it will be apparent from the earlier discussion of the development of pre-school education that in many LEAs provision is very limited and perhaps even non-existent. The Education Act 1980 made it clear that there is no obligation on LEAs to provide nursery education. The only alternative for a child with special needs who requires nursery placement may, therefore, be a special nursery.

Thirdly, Fish (1985) suggests that LEAs may or may not be active in ensuring that parents of children with disabilities are made aware of the importance of early intervention and their legal rights regarding assessment and educational assistance.

Integration and segregation: issues and incidence in pre-school education

> ...I have put forward doubts and questions regarding pre-school intervention for children judged to have special needs. Well founded answers are lacking; rather there would seem to be many articles of faith regarding intervention.
>
> (Davis, 1984)

> It is not proposed to argue the case for early intervention as its value is now a matter of fact.
>
> (Fish, 1985)

Faith or fact? The integration/segregation debate assumes that early intervention is desirable and necessary and the second statement above is more characteristic of current public and official opinion and policy than the first. Davis, however, questions whether nursery placement is always the best solution for a child with special needs and indeed goes further, to suggest that home teaching programmes may not be desirable in every case. It was argued in the previous chapter that researchers have not provided conclusive evidence to support the value of pre-school education. Even less is known about the needs of the pre-school handicapped child and the shift in support away from special schools towards integrated provision would seem to have been motivated by emotional reactions and commonsense theories rather than by research findings highlighting the benefits of integrated education for handicapped children.

Because of this, the literature abounds with contradictions and unsubstantiated claims. Even the Warnock Report is inconsistent in its views. It states that children with impaired hearing need to start their education early and extrapolates this to all children with special needs, advocating that early education is the key to their individual development. Paragraph 5.29 recommends that 'wherever possible measures to stimulate or encourage the early development of children with disabilities ... should be based on the home' and paragraph 5.49 states that 'we believe that young children with special needs can benefit very considerably from nursery education, whether on a full or part time basis, and that wherever possible they should be educated in ordinary nursery schools and classes.'

HOME VISITING SCHEMES

This series is primarily concerned with meeting special needs in ordinary schools but a brief examination of home visiting is necessary, since this form of intervention has expanded rapidly during the past decade and is likely to be experienced by many families with a handicapped pre-school child, especially during the first two years (Aplin and Pugh, 1983).

Home visiting schemes commonly involve regular visits to the homes of children with special needs, often from birth. The visitors, who are frequently trained teachers, advise parents on the handling of their children. The content of the 'educational' programme varies considerably, often depending on the philosophy and style of interaction favoured by the individual visitor (Raven, 1980). Some adopt a strict teaching style in which particular skills will be taught in an ordered sequence. Others will use a less structured approach to encourage general language development and reasoning skills. Some concentrate mainly on working with the child, others work closely with the parents, sometimes acting as counsellor and social worker and always as adviser.

Portage Guide to Early Education

The Portage Guide to Early Education is a home-based early intervention programme which has been widely used in this country since its introduction from the USA in 1976. Developed in rural Wisconsin in 1969, it is a training programme aimed at teaching parents how to teach their pre-school children. The Portage home visitor and parents jointly assess the child's developmental level using a checklist of 580 behaviours. These are organised into stages of development and cover infant stimulation, self-help, motor skills, socialisation, cognitive development and language. Activity cards contain many specific tasks for teaching new behaviours, each card linked to behaviours in the checklist. Target behaviours are selected for each child and the progress of parents and children is assessed regularly. For further details of the Portage scheme and examples of assessment and activity cards, see Wilcock (1981).

For professionals seeking to support parents and help handicap-ped children, the highly structured Portage package was seen as a great boon. Here was a ready-made programme which seemed useful for a wide range of children with special needs. Proponents of the scheme wrote enthusiastically about its success rate and made far-reaching claims about its usefulness and applicability. A National Portage Survey identified 64 such schemes operating in the United Kingdom, concentrated mainly in London, the West Midlands, South Wales and Lancashire (Bendall in Cameron, 1986). The National Foundation for Educational Research, which dissemi-nates the materials in the United Kingdom, produced a series of books supporting the Portage scheme and describing many of the projects which have been set up (Daly *et al.*, 1985; Cameron, 1986; Copley *et al.*, 1986; Hedderley and Jennings, 1987). Lister (1985) went so far as to say that 'there are few other examples of a system which has been so thoroughly evaluated and which has been so enthusiastically received by parents'.

While there may be some truth in the second claim, it is of some concern that there is a paucity of objective research into the effectiveness of Portage and much of the data presented as research material is, in fact, descriptive, subjective and lacking rigour. Many studies do not incorporate control groups (Cunningham, 1986; Evans and Wright, 1987), questionnaires are more widely used to evaluate success than direct observation and assessment (Clements *et al.*, 1982; Frederickson and Haran, 1986; Lorenz, 1987) and there is often bias in the selection of families, with those most highly motivated being involved and, hence, giving positive feedback (Land, 1985). The small scale and short duration of much of the research makes generalisation impossible. The motivation for carrying out a study is often not to evaluate objectively but to find some positive effect which will then attract further funding for the programme (Wiehl and Barrow, 1987).

The above comments are negative and pessimistic. The intention is not to argue, however, that Portage is ineffective and worthless but rather to urge caution in the widespread instigation of any intervention which has not been objectively evaluated. As Lorenz (1987) commented, 'the Portage Bandwaggon, having started to roll, is unwilling to stop'. Ellender (1983) found that children in a Portage programme gained an average of 11 target skills during the period of the study but also acquired at least twice as many other untaught skills during the same period. Cunningham (1986) points to the need for an evaluation of Portage that involves multivariate designs on large numbers of children and families and advocates closer co-ordination of research efforts across establishments using standardised outcome measures. Even Cameron, one of the strongest supporters of the Portage movement, acknowledges that it is not possible to design the perfect evaluation of Portage to answer all the questions, but concludes that 'there is no shame in not knowing, only in not wanting to know' (Cameron, 1986). Certainly there would be little progress in education if we had to wait for research to evaluate every new approach before its implementation. Ongoing evaluation and modification are the keys to innovation but generalisations and the widespread adoption of a particular approach without sound understanding of the processes involved cannot be justified.

Honeylands Home Visiting Project

This home visiting scheme in Exeter, begun in 1975, was less structured than Portage. Honeylands began as a hospital paediatric service that expanded into the community (Pugh and Russell, 1977). Based in a large country house, it offered day-time and short-term residential care to handicapped children. There was growing concern that more needed to be done to help families in the home with handicapped children under nursery age. Developmental home therapists visited the family weekly. They were mainly staff from Honeylands and came from a wide range of disciplines. As well as setting goals and keeping records for the children, they provided a great deal of emotional support and information for parents.

Pugh (1981a, b) summarises some of the main issues to emerge from the Honeylands Home Visiting Project, including the following:

1. The therapists' visits enhanced the mother's natural authority and autonomy with her child. Initially, mothers were slow to accept that they could bring about progress in their child by their own efforts.
2. The pressure on the mother to carry out daily routines with her child could prove intolerable.
3. Strong emotional attachments can develop between isolated mothers and therapists and these must be handled very sensitively.
4. An important part of any home visiting programme has been to involve brothers and sisters and the extended family.

Need for flexibility

Undoubtedly, Portage or a similar home visiting scheme will benefit many families with a handicapped pre-school child. Some families will be identified as unable to cope with their child without assistance, for any number of reasons. Other parents will be capable of coping and providing a stimulating home environment for their handicapped child but will still welcome the support and encouragement of a home visitor. Still others may be able to cope alone and would see a home intervention programme as unnecessary and perhaps even undesirable. A highly structured programme such as Portage may be suitable for parents who need clear-cut guidelines and specific directives but for others it may bring about an unnatural relationship between parent and child. Some parents will be encouraged and strengthened by their new role while others might feel that their confidence is undermined by the regular presence of a professional adviser who seems to be much more knowledgeable.

It is, therefore, clear that flexibility is required when considering provision for the young child with special needs. Each family must be carefully assessed to decide whether educational intervention in the form of home visiting is necessary or desirable. If such a scheme would be welcomed by the family, then the nature of the programme and the degree of structure must be carefully planned to meet the needs of each individual family (Browning *et al.*, 1983).

NURSERY EDUCATION

Few would argue with the view that the baby and very young child with special needs should remain in the home, to be cared for and educated by parents, with or without the support of educational home visitors. Only where conditions in the home environment are extremely unsatisfactory should a small child be removed partly or totally into alternative care and this would apply to all children, the presence or absence of special need being largely irrelevant.

There is considerably less consensus regarding the age at which children, and particularly those with special needs, should begin attendance at a nursery. Children do not generally begin attending nursery schools and classes or playgroups until the age of 3 years. Children with special needs have been admitted to nursery classes in special schools from the age of 2 years and sometimes even earlier. There is no available evidence to suggest the most appropriate age for nursery admission and each child and family must be considered individually. Many factors will determine when a child should be admitted to nursery, including the nature of the child's needs, the ability of the family to meet these needs and the availability of suitable pre-school provision.

The remainder of this chapter will examine pre-school provision for children with special needs, focusing on their integration into mainstream facilities.

SOME DEFINITIONS

There has been a tendency to view special educational provision as a dichotomy – a child is either integrated or segregated. The problem lies in using 'integration' as a state, not a process. A child is 'integrated' if he is placed in an ordinary educational setting regardless of the amount of support he gets or the amount of time he spends there (Booth, 1981). If things go wrong for the child with special needs in the ordinary school, then it is claimed that 'integration' has failed without examining the causes. For example, Cave (1974) reports a survey by Crawford (1972) which outlines as many as 13 difficulties that might be encountered in integrating mentally handicapped children into ordinary nurseries. They all relate to factors within the child (even referring to 'lack of sense of humour') and do not mention other factors.

Hegarty and Pocklington (1981) considered various definitions of integration. They argue that it should refer to a process whereby 'an ordinary school and a special group interact to form a new educational whole' but in real usage this is narrowed. Integration is commonly seen as something done by or to the handicapped child, it being the *child's* problem. It is also frequently used to mean simple associations or links.

Segregation is relatively simple to define. To segregate is 'to set apart, to isolate, to group apart' (MacDonald, 1972). In educational terms, total segregation means educating children with special needs in special schools, which are quite separate from the ordinary school system.

If integration is the process of unification into a whole then that must be the ultimate goal of total educational integration. In practice, however, much so-called integrated and segregated provision will lie somewhere on a continuum between total integration and total segregation. The Warnock Report attempted to clarify the situation by defining three points on this continuum.

1. Location integration. Children with special needs attend special units or classes set up in ordinary schools but have little or no contact with children in the ordinary classes.
2. Social integration. Children attend special units as in (1) above but share social activities with the other children, including eating, playing and out-of-classroom activities.

3. Functional integration. This is the fullest form of integration, closest to the concept of a unified whole, whereby children with special needs experience not only locational and social integration but also participate fully in the educational programmes of the ordinary classroom.

These categories are not definitive since there will in effect be varying degrees of locational integration, of social integration and of functional integration.

INCIDENCE OF INTEGRATION

Statistics

It will be clear from the above definitions of integration that it is very difficult to obtain an accurate picture of the extent of integration at a national level. Statistics relating to numbers of children attending special schools are collated by the government. Children with special needs attending ordinary schools, whether in units or ordinary classes, are considered to be integrated into the ordinary school system. The degree of locational, social and functional integration is not considered. Children in 'integrated' units may be as segregated, and more obviously so, as those in special schools.

The pre-school situation is very difficult to assess. Apart from integrated units for the deaf and partially hearing, which are relatively well-established (Watson, 1973), nursery schools and classes will not produce detailed statistics for children with special needs in attendance. Day nurseries cater for large numbers of children with social, emotional and behaviour problems but they are not geared up to identify and assess other special needs which might be present among their children. Playgroups are even less well equipped to identify special needs and keep no records of this kind on their children.

Surveys

One viable research approach is to conduct a survey of ordinary nursery provision within a given area in order to determine the prevalence of particular special needs among the children in attendance. Two points of caution must be noted, however, concerning this type of data collection. Firstly, the survey generally reveals the perceptions of staff in identifying children as having special needs. Many such children will not, as yet, have been formally assessed. The behaviour of a child in one nursery might be considered a problem but be accepted or tolerated in another nursery where different standards apply. Perceived prevalence of special needs must bear some relation to real prevalence and it may indeed be the case that over-estimations of problems in some nurseries are cancelled out by under-estimations in others. Nevertheless, these remain unknown factors.

Secondly, surveys really only tap evidence of location integration. Detailed interviews with members of staff might reveal much about the organisation of the nursery day and the perceived or purported success of integration but only direct observation of the child in the nursery can present a true picture of the experiences of that child and the actual extent of social and functional integration.

Chazan *et al.* (1980) carried out such a survey in two local authorities in England and Wales in 1976/1977. The initial screening schedule, completed by health visitors, nursery school and class teachers and playgroup leaders, involved the identification of children aged 3 years 9 months to 4 years 3 months within nine categories of special need: vision, hearing, locomotion, muscular control and co-ordination, mental ability, speech and language, social, emotional and behavioural aspects, general health and other. There is no explanation for the omission of day care provision from the survey. Almost one-quarter of all the children in nursery schools and classes or known to health visitors were identified as having one or more special needs. Playgroup leaders identified only 7 per cent of their children in this way. Of all those identified as having special educational needs, less than 5 per cent were found to have severe difficulties (Chazan and Laing, 1982).

By far the most commonly reported special needs which children were 'definitely' and 'possibly' reported to have were behaviour problems (14.5 per cent of all children attending) and speech and language difficulties (12.4 per cent). Physical and mental handicap accounted for only around 6 per cent.

Clark *et al.* (1977) conducted a similar survey for the Warnock Committee in Scotland with a pilot survey being conducted in Central Region and the main survey in Grampian Region. Staff were asked to identify children according to nine categories of special need: visual, auditory, speech, physical and mental handicap, emotional/social, multiple, gifted/talented and other. In Central Region, 14 nursery schools and classes were included, catering for 834 children. Of the children attending 7.5 per cent were perceived as being handicapped and 1.7 per cent as gifted or talented. It must be noted, however, that more than half of the 77 children identified as handicapped or gifted were found in two schools.

In Grampian Region, nursery schools and classes, day nurseries and playgroups were surveyed. Staff identified approximately 6, 17 and 11 per cent respectively of their children as having one or more special needs. As in the Chazan study, speech and language difficulties and behaviour problems accounted for the majority of special needs identified.

The DES funded a post-Warnock follow up of the Scottish survey which was carried out in the West Midlands in 1980/1981 (Clark *et al.*, 1982). Again, nursery schools and classes, day nurseries and playgroups were included, involving a total of 55 pre-school units in Birmingham and 49 in Coventry. The categories of special need used in the Scottish survey were applied, with a few adaptations to suit the West Midlands situation, mainly relating to second language difficulties which had not arisen in the earlier survey.

The perceived incidence of special need in ordinary pre-school units was found to be high, particularly in nursery schools and classes, where as many as 38.3 per cent of children attending were identified in the Birmingham area (see Table 2.1).

As expected, however, some of the figures were considerably inflated by the category of second language difficulty, especially among children in nursery schools and classes and playgroups. When second language problems only were removed, the reported incidence of special need in ordinary nursery schools and classes, playgroups and day nurseries were approximately 17, 7 and 15 per cent, respectively, of the total numbers of children attending.

These figures are meaningless without some information about the severity of the handicapping conditions and so detailed information was obtained from nursery staff regarding the nature and severity of each child's difficulty.

1. Sensory handicap. Those children identified as partially sighted and partially hearing tended to be mildly handicapped. The three exceptions were children with severe hearing loss attending an ordinary nursery class with a small hearing unit attached.
2. Speech and language difficulties. By far the largest category of special needs was speech and language difficulties, even when second language problems were excluded. The problems took the form of speech defects, such as hare lips, stammers and cleft palates, and language difficulties, which were more varied and often found in association with other categories, most frequently behaviour problems and learning difficulties.
3. Physical handicap. Most of the children identified with physical handicap were mildly disabled and capable of coping in the nursery without extra help and support. The most severe

Table 2.1 *Numbers of children and types of special need in nursery schools and classes in the Birmingham research area*

	Nursery schools Number*	%†	Nursery classes Number*	%†
Visual	4	1.3	–	–
Auditory	1	–	4	0.2
Speech	53	21.7	31	5.2
Second language	61	31.8	397	86.5
Physical	29	9.6	6	1.3
Mental	9	1.9	2	0.4
Behaviour	32	12.1	7	1.5
Other	2	0.6	1	–
Gifted	2	0.6	2	0.4
More than one	33	21.0	19	4.1
Total number of children identified	157		459	
Number in units	686		922	
Number of units	9		15	
Percentage identified	22.9		49.8	

*Number, total number of instances of each category, whether singly or with another category or categories.
†%, percentages refer to children identified in each category as compared with total identified.

problems were found in day nurseries and were children aged 2 years and under suffering from spina bifida, cerebral palsy and congenital heart defects who were expected to transfer to special schools at the age of 3 years. Typical physical handicaps identified were controlled epilepsy, eczema, asthma, mild or repaired heart defects, obesity and mild partial paralysis.

4. Learning difficulties. Relatively few children were perceived as having mild, moderate or severe learning difficulties. This probably reflects the view that unless a child has a readily identifiable condition causing mental retardation, such as Down's Syndrome, staff feel unable or unwilling to attach this label to children at such an early age. Only two children with Down's Syndrome attended the units visited, one in a day nursery and the other in a nursery school. Plans were already underway to move the latter child to a special school because, although he was described as active, cheerful, toilet

trained and socially integrated, his short concentration span was placing too many demands on staff.

5. Behaviour problems. Behaviour problems accounted for the second highest rate of referral. Nursery schools and classes tended to refer children as being under-reactive, defined as being withdrawn, timid and fearful of new experiences and other children. Day nurseries identified relatively more children as over-reactive, being aggressive, noisy, domineering, bullying and resistant to adult control. Day nursery staff attributed this to the fact that many of the children in attendance came from poor home environments where parental control was lacking.

6. Giftedness. Staff frequently stated that they found it impossible to say whether a child was gifted at pre-school age. Giftedness, like learning difficulties, seemed to be equated with academic achievement, which could not be assessed until the child had attempted several years of formal education. Identification of giftedness was found to be particularly subjective. For example, a child of German and English parents was identified as gifted because he spoke both languages fluently, but several equally bilingual Asian children in the same nursery class were not so perceived! Another nursery class teacher provided detailed information about the skills of a gifted child in her unit, describing his advanced behaviour both at school and at home. When pressed as to how she knew so much about the home life of this gifted child, it emerged that he was her grandson! These examples highlight the need for face-to-face interviews in collecting survey information rather than reliance on written questionnaires.

7. Multiple handicap. Only four children were perceived to be multiply handicapped (being placed in three or more categories of special need). Two attended nursery schools and two were in day nurseries. They were all aged 3 years and over and were all awaiting special nursery places.

It will be seen that the categories above, with the exception of giftedness, were all considered by the Warnock Report. This extensive survey revealed that very few children attending the ordinary pre-school units visited were perceived as having severe handicapping conditions. The majority of children identified had speech and language difficulties and behaviour problems. Those children who did suffer from physical and mental disabilities were often about to be transferred to special school nurseries.

The conclusion which must be drawn from the above surveys is that ordinary pre-school units were catering for children with relatively mild handicapping conditions. If children with more complex special needs were receiving nursery education, this must have been in special nursery provision.

SEGREGATED PRE-SCHOOL PROVISION

Segregated pre-school provision is usually found in nursery classes attached to special schools. Admission to such classes can generally take place at an earlier age than to ordinary nursery classes, often from 2 years. The West Midlands research project (Clark *et al.*, 1982) included surveys of special education to determine the nature of the provision and the characteristics of the children attending. Some of the findings are outlined below.

Types of nursery class

All 12 nursery classes attached to special schools in Birmingham were visited. Six nursery classes were attached to special schools for children with learning difficulties and three to schools for the physically handicapped. It was noted, however, that this distinction was not so clearly made in the nursery units of these schools. Most of the physically handicapped schools contained pre-school children with learning difficulties and vice versa. It is often difficult to determine a child's major handicapping condition and to assess the severity of his or her handicap at the age of 2 years. Assessment and diagnosis would, therefore, be carried out in a special nursery class and, if necessary, a child would be transferred to a more suitable school at the age of 5 or 6 years.

Of the remaining three nursery units, one was attached to a school for the deaf, all the children in this class having hearing problems and some having additional special needs. The second nursery class was within a school for maladjusted children and was attended by pre-school children with various special needs, many due to social deprivation and poor home circumstances. All of these children transferred to other schools at the age of 5 years since they were not assessed as 'maladjusted' (furthermore, maladjusted children were not admitted to this school until the age of 8 years and so there was no infant department). The final nursery unit in Birmingham was part of a school for children with severe learning difficulties and catered for pre-school children with multiple handicaps.

There were six nursery classes attached to special schools in Coventry, three in schools for children with severe learning difficulties, one in a school for moderate learning difficulties and two in schools for the physically handicapped.

Special nursery classes were, therefore, very varied and professed to cater for a wide range of special needs, often within the same class. Information was obtained from head teachers to determine the characteristics of the children in attendance.

Numbers of children and age range

A total of 138 children attended the special nursery classes in Birmingham, 93 aged 4 years and under and the remaining 45 children being 5 years of age and over. Eight to ten-year-old 'nursery' children were found in one school where handicapping conditions were so severe that the children were functioning at pre-school level and so a nursery place was felt to be most appropriate. In other schools such children were placed in special care units, separate from the under-fives. Similarly, in the units in Coventry, approximately half of the 57 children were of pre-school age, the remainder being 5 and 6 years old, with only two children over 6 years of age.

Nature of special needs

The following findings relate to the pre-school age children (4 years old and under). Within classes for the physically handicapped, 17 children were reported to suffer from spina bifida, the severity ranging from a child who was immobile and doubly incontinent to those who walked and were mildly incontinent. Twenty-five children suffered from cerebral palsy. Three children with brittle bones had no other special needs. A 3-year-old Asian child attended a nursery class for the hearing impaired and was perceived to be of superior intellectual ability. Several children suffered from relatively rare syndromes which affected the neurological system and body metabolism, including Batten's Disease, Leish–Nyhan Syndrome and calcium imbalance in the brain. The consequences of these conditions are varied, including defective motor co-ordination, sensory ability and mental functioning, epilepsy and compulsive self-mutilation.

Pre-school children in special nursery classes for learning difficulties fell into two main groups: those with a known physical or genetic abnormality and those in whom the causes were less apparent, involving diffuse brain damage and/or social and emotional deprivation resulting in severely delayed development.

Twenty children were found to have Down's Syndrome. Approximately half of these children suffered mild to severe learning difficulty, were mobile and could engage in a wide range of nursery activities. The remainder were more severely debilitated. For example, a 4-year-old boy with visual handicap and a club foot had a serious heart defect which rendered him immobile on a cushion on the nursery floor. Four other children with Down's Syndrome respectively suffered convulsions and varying degrees of brain damage, arrested hydrocephalus and microcephalus/tetraplegia. Finally, a 3-year-old boy with Down's Syndrome was multiply handicapped since he suffered five epileptic fits daily and had a congenital abnormality of the hip joints. Down's Syndrome is not, therefore, a suitable term to describe such children. They all manifest the chromosomal abnormality which signifies Down's Syndrome but there is considerable variation in their ability to function and to acquire new skills.

Nursery children over 5 years of age

Of the 195 children in special nursery classes 72 were aged 5 years and over. As discussed previously, their attendance was due to the fact that the children were still functioning at pre-school level. By definition, they were severely handicapped. For example, an epileptic 8-year-old had a grossly abnormal EEG and virtually no motor ability. The oldest child in a nursery unit was a 10-year-old boy with athetoid cerebral palsy, microcephaly, epilepsy and a visual defect. Ten of the children in this age group had Down's Syndrome and most were around 5 or 6 years old and about to move on to another class.

Nursery children with minimal special needs

At the opposite end of the scale were children whose special needs were minimal, for whom ordinary nursery education would seem more appropriate and even imperative. Four children suffering from Perthes' Disease had made marked improvement and teachers felt that their transfer to ordinary education was overdue. Several children were retarded due to poor home circumstances and staff hoped that they would attend ordinary infant school. Some 5- and 6-year-olds in a nursery class for children with mild learning difficulties were labelled 'slow learners' and their teacher felt that they would cope in an ordinary school with some support. In the same class was a 5-year-old boy who had been removed from ordinary school because of behaviour problems. He had no learning difficulties. A 4-year-old girl had been placed in a nursery class for the physically handicapped because she was labelled 'hyperactive'. The class catered for severely handicapped children with brain damage, spina bifida, epilepsy and paralysis.

Two children with no special needs were found in special nursery classes, both placed there at the request of parents who wanted them to accompany handicapped siblings. One girl of 3 years of age attended with her 4-year-old brother, who had severe learning difficulties and no speech. The other children in this class were emotionally disturbed and/or had severe learning difficulties. The second child was placed in a class for multiply handicapped children with a physically handicapped sibling.

PLACEMENT DECISIONS

The findings from the above surveys of ordinary and special nursery provision have been presented in some detail because they highlight some of the major issues in the integration/segregation debate.

It is impossible to obtain an accurate national picture of the extent of integration of children with special needs at pre-school level. Relevant statistics are not collated and placement policy, resources and the nature of pre-school provision vary considerably from one local authority to another. It appears, however, that even within a local authority there is no rationale governing decisions to place children in ordinary or special provision. On the whole, children in ordinary facilities would fall within the sphere of moderate to minimal special needs on a continuum of severity while the most severely disabled children were found in special nursery classes. There is considerable overlap, however, and a broad grey area in the middle where children could be placed in either category.

The descriptions of the conditions and needs of some of the children in special nurseries support the view put forward in the Warnock Report that 'special schools will continue to feature prominently in the range of provisions for children with special educational needs ... [they] will always be required to give some children with special educational needs the benefit of special facilities, teaching methods or expertise ... which cannot reasonably be provided in ordinary schools' (paragraph 8.1).

The special schools included in the survey were categorised according to needs, distinguishing particularly between children with physical handicap and those with learning difficulties. In the nursery classes, however, children with differing needs seemed to be put together randomly. It was noted that some children will have varied needs and that the needs of others will not have been fully assessed and diagnosed. It is a common complaint of many parents of physically handicapped children, however, that they have more in common socially, cognitively and linguistically with normal children than with children who have learning difficulties. Indeed, many LEAs do not distinguish between physical handicap and learning difficulties and provide only combined schools. It is also of some concern that children with behaviour problems should be sent to inappropriate special schools.

The diversity of special needs within a nursery class is further exacerbated by the wide age-range which was found in many units, with 'nursery' children being aged 2–10 years. Older children with very severe handicapping conditions were, therefore, placed with younger children whose needs were relatively less severe.

The range of children placed in a nursery class meant that for many children there was no real peer group stimulation to encourage cognitive and linguistic development and social skills. It was interesting that the teachers in the two classes which contained a 'normal' child both stated that the presence of that child greatly increased the level of functioning and general alertness of all the children and changed the whole ethos of the class.

These, then, are some of the negative aspects of segregated pre-school provision. There have, of course, been positive reasons for opting for special nurseries and these relate mainly to resources. Structured interviews were carried out with staff in all the ordinary and special nurseries in the West Midlands study to discover more about the nature of the provision and the viability of meeting special needs. As would be expected, resources to meet special needs were superior in specialised nurseries. Resources included staffing (training and staff/child ratios), accommodation, special teaching aids and materials and the accessibility of a wide range of professional advisers and support staff. No more will be said here about these factors since the remainder of this book will be concerned with the means of making the excellent resources of the special nursery available to children with special needs in ordinary nurseries.

—3————————————————————

Planned learning in the nursery

————————————————————

> Where a child who has special needs is being educated in an ordinary
> school maintained by a local education authority it shall be the duty of
> those concerned with making special educational provision for that
> child to secure ... that the child engages in the activities of the school
> together with children who do not have special educational needs.
> (Education Act 1981, Paragraph 2.7.)

The first section of this book has attempted to determine the extent
of locational integration. We now move on to discuss the social and
functional integration of children with special needs into ordinary
nursery schools, classes and centres. The obvious starting point for
such a discussion would be to ascertain typical features of the
ordinary nursery environment and then to examine the means
whereby children with special needs can be fully involved within
this environment. As with the examination of locational integration,
this task is not straightforward because of the very nature of
pre-school education. I would argue that it is necessary to take a
much broader perspective of the nursery environment than simply
to examine the activities which are offered, as suggested in the
above quotation from the 1981 Act.

The overall aims of nursery education must be applicable to
children with special needs. The objectives of the nursery curriculum must be fully stated to reflect these aims and to be relevant to
the needs of all children. A clear understanding of how young
children learn will indicate the most appropriate means of obtaining
these objectives. It is only within this framework that the specific
activities in the nursery can be understood and seen to be relevant or
otherwise.

Encompassing children with special needs within the aims and
objectives of the nursery curriculum is much more important than
simply ensuring that they can take part in specific activities. If
attitudes towards integration are positive at all levels of the
pre-school hierarchy, from officials at the DES through the local
authority to the practitioners in the nurseries, then children with
special needs will be accommodated within the aims and objectives
of the nursery curriculum. Ensuring that suitable activities and
materials are available is a relatively minor problem. After all, the

ethos of the nursery environment, with its emphasis on informality and flexibility, should make integration at pre-school level an easier task than at higher levels of education, which have traditionally been associated with formality, timetabling and a structured curriculum.

In this chapter, the pre-school curriculum will be considered in terms of the aims and objectives of nursery education. The learning mechanisms of young children will be discussed and related to the degree of structure required within the nursery setting and the role of the adult. The nursery environment and activities will be discussed. Once we have a clearer picture of what adults think children should be doing and learning in the nursery and how they should be filling their time, we will focus attention on what children actually do in this environment by means of findings from observational studies. A limited amount of observational research has focused on the child with special needs in the ordinary nursery.

This research will provide guidelines for ensuring that social and functional integration are maximised for children with special needs. Indeed, it will be argued that some modifications in the nursery routine will benefit all children.

PLANNED LEARNING IN THE NURSERY

Consideration of the curriculum in relation to pre-school education has often been too narrow. It is frequently used only as a description of the nursery experience for a child in terms of specific activities and materials used. Content and subject matter are, however, only a part of the curriculum and are dependent on the aims, objectives and outline programme of activities (Hirst, 1969). Taylor (1970) outlines the following steps in planning a curriculum:

1. Deciding on *general aims* of education for the children concerned.
2. Analysing the aims into *general objectives* which indicate desired skills and behaviours to be achieved.
3. Analysing general objectives into *specific objectives* which break down skills and behaviours into component parts.
4. Identifying *learning experiences and activities* that will help children to achieve specific objectives.

There has been a reluctance or an inability throughout the development of pre-school education to define clearly the nursery curriculum in the above terms. As we shall see, broad aims were often stated reflecting the perspective of the pre-school pioneer or the prevailing attitude of society towards pre-school provision, but these aims did not generally lead to carefully analysed objectives and activities. Pre-school curriculum development has indeed been hindered by divergent views of the desirability of nursery education and of the regime that is most suitable for pre-school children. Conversely, failure to identify a curriculum gave rise to an unfortunately negative view of the impact of nursery education. This is summed up in Blank's much quoted description of the nursery school as 'a secure, benign environment' where children follow their own instincts within a *laissez-faire* regime (Blank, 1974).

I would put forward five important reasons for thoroughly planning a pre-school curriculum:

1. If aims and objectives are not identified there can be no rationale for the activities offered to the child and consequently there is a danger that the nursery environment becomes cluttered with materials which have limited educational value.
2. Short and long-term objectives allow the content of the curriculum to be spread out over time (Gulliford, 1971). New materials and activities can be introduced in an organised way to meet the changing needs of the children.
3. The aims and general objectives for children with special needs will be the same as for ordinary children in the nursery but consideration of specific objectives must be tailored to meet the specific needs which a child presents. Attention will then be focused on suitable activities and materials to ensure that the child fulfils these objectives.
4. Evaluation depends on assessing outcomes in terms of their approximation to the goals which were set. Clark (1979) argues strongly that evaluation of a nursery unit is only meaningful if it is examined in the context of *its own* aims and not aims which others think it might or should have. Without evidence of common goals in pre-school education, it is impossible to make global evaluations. This has been the fault of much pre-school research, as discussed in previous chapters. I would add that evaluation of an integration exercise is equally meaningless if aims and objectives have not been established.
5. Research has shown that staff behaviour can be influenced by the avowed educational aims, or lack of them, that predominate in a unit (Tizard *et al.*, 1976a).

A recent publication is devoted entirely to the pre-school curriculum and the author argues that 'there is a recognisable curriculum for children under statutory school age based on skills and competencies to be developed in a flexible and child-centred environment' (Curtis, 1986). A closer examination of the curriculum now follows.

AIMS OF NURSERY EDUCATION

No British government publication has attempted to lay down explicit, common aims for nursery education in this country. The aims of the early pioneers of nursery provision centred upon the value of nursery attendance in compensating for the inadequacies in children's home experiences. The deficit model still has some relevance but it is more popular today to view nursery experience as complementary to everything else that happens to a child, rather than compensatory.

Philosophers of education can identify broad conceptions of education which produce very different aims. Lloyd (1983) describes the utilitarian view of education, which demands that outcomes be related to practical demands in the real world. Education is not for education's sake. Applied to nursery education, this stance would incorporate such aims as laying the foundations of literacy and numeracy (Clark, 1983b) and preparing the child for later stages of education. The egalitarian would still adhere to the deficit model and see the aim of nursery education as providing equal opportunities for all, thereby helping to reduce inequalities in society.

Others have attempted to identify more specific aims. In the first major study of the aims of nursery education, Taylor *et al.* (1972) concentrated on five relatively specific aims, defined as intellectual development, social and emotional development, aesthetic development, physical development and the creation of an effective transition from home to school. These are general objectives rather than aims, derived from the liberal view of education which places the greatest emphasis on personal development and the engendering of self-autonomy.

It follows from this emphasis on personal development and the maximising of individual potential that similar liberal aims for education should apply to all levels within the educational system. Continuity in education is a much discussed topic at the present time. Education begins at birth. The aims of education should, therefore, be the same for the home teacher working with children in the early months as for the secondary teacher. Relating this philosophy to early education, Webb (1974) succinctly defines education as meaning:

> that process by which an individual is aided by informed instruction, guidance, demonstration, provision and opportunity to pursue

worthwhile activities to as high a degree of critical awareness and
rational autonomy as possible to him.

(p. 58)

It is obvious that this general aim for pre-school education readily
encompasses all children in a unit, regardless of individual
differences and the existence of special needs. From this statement
of aims can be derived general objectives which define areas for
development and consequently lead on to identification of 'worthwhile activities' to meet these objectives.

OBJECTIVES OF NURSERY EDUCATION

The general objectives should encompass all those spheres of a
child's development which can be nurtured in the nursery
environment. We have already noted the five main objectives
studied by Taylor *et al.* (1972). The literature abounds with
alternative suggestions. Curtis (1986) outlines seven areas for
attention, namely self-awareness, social skills, cultural awareness,
communication skills, motor and perceptual abilities, analytical and
problem-solving skills and aesthetic and creative awareness. She
would add to this the need to develop a child's natural curiosity and
encourage intrinsic motivation.

The above list highlights some important aspects of pre-school
objectives. Firstly, the categories are not mutually exclusive. There
is a danger that such categorisation of skills can lead to the artificial
isolation of one area of development from another and so staff must
fully discuss the overlaps which exist and the implications of these.
Secondly, while there are general objectives for pre-school education which apply to all units, there are other objectives which will be
relevant only to particular units at particular times. For example, the
engendering of cultural awareness will have more pressing
significance in pre-school units in the West Midlands than in the
North of Scotland, where the integration of children from a variety
of cultural backgrounds is not a feature of nursery education (Clark
et al., 1977). Thirdly, not only will nursery units need to list
objectives in terms of priority, but the varying needs of the children
in the unit will also require that individual priorities are considered.
The child who is emotionally disturbed will not make progress
intellectually or socially until behaviour problems receive attention.
Motor and perceptual abilities will be a major priority for children
with physical difficulties. For some children, priorities will be
obvious and directly related to their identifiable special needs. For
others with complex needs, careful observation and assessment will

be required to determine priorities.

In summary, then, the general objectives of the nursery unit will be applicable to all children but priorities for individual children will differ according to their most pressing needs at any one time. The great advantage of clearly defining objectives is that children's areas of strength, as well as their weaknesses, can be identified. It can also be ensured that, although particular children may need extra help and more time spent within one area of the curriculum, other areas of development are not neglected. This avoids the danger, often characteristic of segregated education, of seeing the child in terms of his or her diagnosed handicapping conditions and focusing too much attention on these skills to the detriment of overall development.

It is clear that objectives for nursery education must be determined at grass roots level and must involve discussions with all nursery practitioners. General objectives can be worked out by pre-school advisers within the LEA in collaboration with head teachers and pre-school support services but they cannot be implemented without consultation with all teachers, nursery nurses and nursery assistants. This will give a framework and a rationale for the things that are actually done in the nursery. Similarly, specific objectives and priorities for individual children will need to be drawn up by nursery staff, professional advisers and parents; the details of this will be discussed in later chapters.

It might be helpful at this point to illustrate the steps that must be taken in order to go from general to specific objectives. To take an example from Curtis (1986), a general objective is stated as the development of social skills. Within this category, she defines specific objectives as (a) affiliation skills, (b) co-operation and the resolution of conflict and (c) kindness, care and affection. On the basis of these specific objectives, suitable materials and activities can be devised.

HOW DO PRE-SCHOOL CHILDREN LEARN?

Educational aims and objectives cannot be put into practice without a clear understanding of how children learn. There is no definitive theory which fully explains the mechanisms of learning but the greatest single influence on educational practice in this century has unquestionably been Jean Piaget.

Piagetian theories of learning

The pre-school child in the nursery is functioning within the preoperational period of development, which emphasises the child's struggle to represent the world through language, in preparation for the period of concrete operations. Piaget views the child as an active learner who is constantly trying to make sense of the world and achieve a comfortable level of harmony with the environment. This concept of harmony or equilibrium compels the child to assimilate and accommodate new information into his or her existing schemas. The child is therefore stimulated to learn by the challenges of his environment. That does not mean that *every* activity must be difficult and challenging. As Blank (1972) comments, if this were the case the child would see the nursery experience 'only as a situation in which he is required to do all the things that he is least capable of doing. From this point of view, he stands only to lose.' Rather, the usefulness of Piaget's concept of equilibrium lies in the fact that it heightens awareness of the value of the activities which are offered. For example, most nursery units provide the child with a sand tray. During initial encounters with this new material, the child will experiment and actively learn about the properties of wet and dry sand, but if the materials do not change and several months later the child is still using the sand in much the same way, then staff must be aware that very little new learning is taking place.

The social interaction and stimulation of the school environment are seen as significant for the development of intelligence (Sigel, 1969). Piaget (1963) stated that:

> The human being is immersed right from birth in a social environment which affects him just as much as his physical environment. Society, even more, in a sense, than the physical environment, changes the very structure of the individual, because it not only compels him to recognise facts, but also provides him with a ready-made system of signs, which modify his thought.
>
> (p. 156)

This proposition strongly favours the integration of children with special needs into the more stimulating, social environment of the ordinary nursery unit. Moreover, it focuses attention on the importance of peer group stimulation as a means of developing new skills in a child and so it is advocated that this should be specifically incorporated into the objectives of the nursery curriculum. If a child's special needs make it difficult for him to form relationships with other children and become an active member of the group, then staff must see it as their role to facilitate social interactions. This theme will be developed in later chapters.

Egocentrism

Central to Piaget's conception of the young child was his view that the child is egocentric and unable to adopt the viewpoint or role of others. The famous 'mountains experiment' (Piaget and Inhelder, 1956) is frequently cited to support the theory of early egocentrism. In the mountains experiment children were asked to imagine the view a doll would have when placed in different positions around a mountain scene in which one mountain had a cross on top, another was snow-capped and a third had a house on top. Children communicated their responses in several ways, for example by selecting one picture from a group of pictures to show how the mountains would look from the doll's perspective or selecting one picture and placing the doll in the correct position so that it would see the identical view. Piaget and Inhelder produced evidence to show that 6-year-old children show some awareness of the perspective of others but decentrism is not mastered until the age of 9 years. The social context of the pre-school and infant class plays an important part in helping the child to decentre (Light, 1979). 'With confrontation from social agents (peers, teachers, parents) as well as the inanimate environment, the child acquires an objectified view of self and the world around him' (Sigel, 1969).

It is well known that more recent research has cast doubt on Piaget's view that the pre-school child is totally egocentric. For example, Hughes (1975; and in Donaldson, 1978) devised the 'policeman' experiment. Two walls intersected to form a cross. One policeman doll was placed so that he could 'see' two of the four open areas marked B and D in Figure 1 and another policeman was placed so that he could see areas A and B. The child was asked to hide a little boy doll so that the policemen could not see him (in area C).

Ninety per cent of the 3½–5-year-olds in Hughes's study gave correct responses and even the youngest children, with average age 3 years 9 months, obtained an 88 per cent success rate. Hughes made the task more complex with six sections and three policemen and still obtained success with pre-schoolers (60 per cent of 3-year-olds and 90 per cent of 4-year-olds).

Borke (1983) devised three-dimensional scenes to assess egocentrism. The simplest display consisted of a lake, a miniature of a horse and cow and a model of a house. The second display was a replica of Piaget and Inhelder's mountains. The third display was more complex and contained cowboys, Indians and trees, a lake, a windmill and a variety of farm buildings, people and animals. The child sat at one of the four sides of the display and Grover, a Sesame Street character, was placed at one of the other three sides. A duplicate of the scene was placed beside the child on a turntable and the child had to turn it to indicate the view which Grover would have of the scene. The first display elicited correct responses from 3- and 4-year-old children in 80 per cent of the trials. Similar

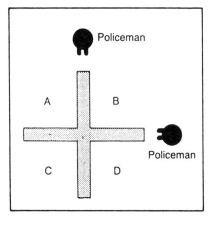

CHILD

Figure 3.1 *Hughes's (1975) policemen and dolls task – layout as viewed from above*

high success rates were obtained on the third display but the mountains scene produced 42 per cent and 67 per cent correct responses from 3- and 4-year-olds respectively.

These studies indicate that children can decentre and take the view of another person if the task is meaningful, if they understand the instructions and if they are given a suitable means of responding. Even the mountains experiment was possible for some pre-school children when Grover was introduced to the scene and the turntable response was used. This does not detract from the role of the nursery in the socialisation of the child and, indeed, suggests that the pre-school child is capable of relatively sophisticated role play. Nursery staff might like to replicate these studies themselves, perhaps using characters from the *Postman Pat* series of books by Cunliffe, which are highly attractive and familiar to the present generation of pre-school children.

Too often the theories of Piaget are read as second-hand, potted versions. Piaget provided a whole thought system which takes considerable study and effort to understand fully. It is only to be expected that new research will produce findings that cause us to modify some of Piaget's views and Piaget himself would have wanted this to be so. There is still, however, great value in returning to Piaget's original writings to obtain a clear understanding of cognitive development in childhood (Smith, 1985). As claimed by Kohlberg (1972) in relation to pre-school education, a Piagetian conception of methods of accelerating intellectual development (employing cognitive conflict, match and sequential ordering of experience), a Piagetian focus upon basic intellectual operations and a Piagetian procedure of assessment of general intellectual development might generate somewhat more general and long-range cognitive effects than would other approaches.

Some critics of Piaget would argue that he was not particularly interested in education and the practical development of the skills and concepts which he described. More recent researchers have attempted to fill this gap by providing theories of how the child learns and grows, based on Piaget's conceptions of child thought and developmental stages. For example, Bruner describes the child's interactions with his environment as progressing from representation through action to representation through pictures and finally to representation through symbols and words. These three media he calls enactive, iconic and symbolic respectively (Bruner *et al.*, 1966; Bruner, 1981). Bruner does not see these 'stages' as following one after the other with previous stages being abandoned; rather the child builds up a repertoire of responses to his environment and so has more options and strategies. McNally (1981) discusses the intuitive (perceptual) stage which characterises the thought of nursery age children and points out that this stage is dominated by 'immediate perceptions, by the dominant aspect of what is attended to, and by the fact that he is unable to keep in mind more than one relation at a time'. This helps to explain the pre-school child's ability to contradict himself repeatedly in language and deed without showing any concern for these inconsistencies and has implications for nursery staff.

Marion Blank applied a cognitive-developmental system to the understanding of language acquisition. In this system the child progresses from concrete to abstract modes of language and communication through four levels which Blank calls matching perception, selective analysis of perception, re-ordering perception and reasoning about perception (Blank *et al.*, 1978; Blank and Franklin, 1980). This model provides useful guidelines for the management and assessment of language and communication in the nursery and will be discussed further in the next chapter.

More attention should be paid by researchers to the early cognitive development of children with special needs. It seems reasonable to assume that the physically disabled child whose mobility is restricted may have had inadequate opportunity to interact actively with his or her environment, to explore and manipulate objects and events. These gaps in experience must be filled to promote cognitive development. This would also be true of children with sensory handicap. Learning difficulties and developmental delay, by definition, imply slow cognitive growth and the need for extra help to be given to acquire new concepts and schemas. For practical purposes, it would seem appropriate to consider children with special needs as following the same pattern of growth and development as normal children, but at a different rate. Some skills will be acquired at the expected time, others will be delayed and may require intervention by the nursery staff. Assessment and observation of each child will produce a profile of strengths and weaknesses in relation to cognitive development.

Theories of cognitive development focus on processes within the child and help us to understand what the child brings to the learning environment. They provide guidelines about how the child thinks and how he or she might react to particular events and challenges which are encountered. Having considered internal processes, it will now be useful to examine external factors and to consider the learning process in action. What are the features of the child's environment that promote learning? The complex topic of play in the nursery will be discussed and extended to consider behavioural approaches to learning, such as imitation, modelling and peer tutoring.

PLAY IN THE NURSERY

> The function of play has been commented on for many centuries to little avail.
>
> Goffman (1976)

Many volumes have been devoted to the study and understanding of children's play. Throughout the centuries it has been observed that all children play. Cross-cultural studies have revealed that play is universal and contains many common principles. Ethologists, biologists and comparative psychologists inform us that all higher species of animals engage in play activities and that these have a purpose in terms of the animal's survival. Developmental and child psychologists accept that play in the young child may appear frivolous but 'it has to have a proper, serious explanation. It cannot just be; it has to have a purpose' (Cohen, 1987). In spite of extensive research endeavours, however, the above statement by Goffman still holds true. Sutton-Smith and Kelly-Byrne (1984) highlight numerous approaches adopted in play research and conclude that 'researchers have been more inclined to give the concept support than to define it carefully'. Lack of rigorous methods for examining play is one reason for this failure to explain it. The application of ethological methods to the study of children's behaviour certainly produced a rich abundance of descriptive material but this only threw up more hypotheses (Blurton-Jones, 1972). It may be that MacDougall (1919) was correct when he said that 'the motives of play are various and often complex and they cannot be characterised by any brief formula' (cited in Cohen, 1987).

The functions of play

The pioneers of pre-school education had very differing and definite views on the role of play, based on their philosophies of education and society rather than empirical observation. For example, for Froebel 'play is the highest level of child development. It is the spontaneous expression of thought and feeling – an expression which his inner life requires' (Lilley, 1967). Play, therefore, deserved careful attention and promotion in the Froebelian nursery environment. Montessori argued that play should only be encouraged if it developed new skills and concepts and so imaginative and fantasy play were excluded from her curriculum. Margaret McMillan and Susan Isaacs both disagreed and placed considerable emphasis on the child's need to engage in imaginary play.

Groos in 1896 was probably the first to express the idea that play leads to learning by allowing the 'pre-exercise' of the skills needed in adulthood. This view of the importance of play for cognitive development is widely accepted today. Hutt (1970) describes the epistemic or exploratory phase of a child's play, during which learning and problem-solving is taking place. This is similar to the complex play described by Sylva *et al.* (1980), involving concentration, goal-directedness and the acquisition of new skills.

Some researchers have focused on play as an aid to social development. Children learn to interact with each other and form relationships through play and may gain some intrinsic satisfaction from being able to control the behaviour of others through episodes of imaginative and fantasy play (Garvey, 1983). Hutt (1970) sees imaginative or ludic play as inferior to epistemic play, since she argues that the former does not lead to learning, but she concedes that it may have some value for the child in allowing the expression of mood and hidden talents. Sylva *et al.* (1980) agree that such 'simple' play may have 'non-intellectual' benefits, such as permitting relaxation and giving the children the opportunity to chat. Much of the research into the social aspects of play was stimulated by the work of Parten (1932), who categorised children's play into solitary, parallel and group depending on the degree of involvement of peers. This categorisation, which has stood the test of time, has been applied widely (Wintre and Webster, 1974; Smith, 1978) and is a useful tool for measuring the social integration of children with special needs.

Play has also been described as a means of helping the child to develop values (Hartley, 1971) and has been credited with, or blamed for, encouraging the development of sex role stereotyping (Dunn and Morgan, 1987).

In response to all of these scientific, practical theories, Cohen (1987) pleads for a less utilitarian view and argues that 'to be worth studying, play does not always have to be *for* something else'. The intrinsic value of play for the child must also be seen in terms of the pure joy and satisfaction which it brings (Cazden, 1983). For the child, the act of playing is its own reward. The child is free from restraints, can experiment without risk of failure and can 'let off steam' to prevent the build-up of frustration (Jeffree *et al.*, 1977).

In summary, play cannot be seen as being cognitive *or* social *or* emotional. It serves all of these purposes. Sometimes the importance of one aspect of development will be more apparent in a particular play bout but just as often, when children play, they will combine all three.

Play deficit

It was stated above that all children play but this belief has been qualified by some researchers, who point out that some children play at an inferior level and so manifest a 'play deficit'. Smilansky (1968) was the first researcher to report this finding, based on work with socially disadvantaged children in Israel. Consequently, it was argued that play was a skill that could be taught and numerous studies were carried out which aimed to make up this deficit by tutoring play skills, thereby improving the children's level of cognitive functioning. Smith and Syddall (1978) reviewed this area of research and carried out their own, more closely controlled, study of play tutoring with fourteen 3- and 4-year-olds. They concluded that the results obtained in most of the studies reviewed could be due to the tutoring aspect of play tutoring rather than the play aspect. In other words, improved performance was brought about by the close adult–child interaction required in the tutoring sessions. This does not necessarily negate the usefulness of play tutoring but rather has wide implications for the role of the adult in the nursery, a theme which will be developed throughout this book.

Play and children with special needs

The topic of play in the context of special needs has received relatively little attention from researchers. The trend towards integration has, however, provided some impetus for such studies. Staff in ordinary nurseries need to be advised on how to encourage play in a child who has special needs. Indeed some staff need to be informed that children with special needs *can* engage in free play since 'the spontaneous behaviours of disabled children fail to live up to people's expectations of what constitutes proper play' (McConkey, 1986). Special education has tended to emphasise the use of direct teaching to develop specific skills which are identified as lacking. Consequently, free play is often seen as wasted time in the special nursery and not scheduled into the daily programme (Widerstrom, 1986).

Several useful reviews have examined research into the play of handicapped children (Mogford, 1977; Quinn and Rubin, 1984; McConkey, 1985). A number of studies have highlighted the importance of spontaneous play for children with special needs (Horne and Philleo, 1976; Sylva *et al.*, 1976). Frequently, researchers have found that they have to initiate play with children who have learning difficulties but once they are engaged, the length of time these children spend on activities could be as long as with normal children.

The study of physically handicapped children has been dominated by medical aspects of their conditions. Consequently, 'the play of such children has received negligible attention. Many types of physical impairment, including deafness, cerebral palsy and muscular dystrophy have been totally ignored in this regard' (Quinn and Rubin, 1984). The play of blind children has received some attention (Sandler and Wills, 1965; Tait, 1972), as has the play of language-delayed children (Lovell *et al.*, 1968).

A recurrent theme throughout the literature on play and exceptional children is the need for adult intervention, even in spontaneous play activities. This may only involve initiating the play session and withdrawing, but it may also require the adult to become more involved in the entire play episode. Staff are very reluctant to become involved in fantasy play. If they do try to take part, they tend to dominate the interaction rather than facilitate. Robson (1983) discussed radio microphone recordings of a nursery nurse in a nursery school who demonstrated how an adult can become involved in a child's fantasy play by role-playing and can encourage the flow of complex language. In the following excerpt the nursery nurse is pretending to be a child and Jane is her 'mother'.

Child: Do you want to make a snowman?
N.N.:   Yes, aren't you going to help me make a snowman?
Child: And don't you get all wet.
N.N.:   No, all right.

Child: I expect you need your mac on.
N.N.:   Oh, all right.
Child: You've got to 'ave your mac on.
N.N.:   Do I have to put my mac on top of my coat or do I have to take my coat off now?
Child: You'll have to take your coat off. Now put your mac on.
N.N.:   Right. Excuse me!
Child: What?
N.N.:   My buttons.
Child: I can't keep coming out 'ere. There you are.
N.N.:   Thank you.

This play episode lasted for 20 minutes, involving up to six children, and it is difficult to capture the quality of the interactions in a short extract. The nursery nurse was not controlling the play but she was teaching the children a great deal by enriching the quality of their dialogue.

Some would advocate a more structured approach to the teaching of symbolic play since this is seen as an important prerequisite of expressive language (e.g. Jeffree *et al.*, 1977). Quinn and Rubin (1984) point to the importance of play in the diagnosis, assessment and treatment of exceptional children. They also stress, however, the need for more rigorous research and improved methodology in this area.

Appendix 2 provides some useful references, resources and addresses to give staff ideas about play materials for pre-school children, particularly those with special needs.

PLAY OBSERVED

Numerous writers and researchers during the past century have contributed to our knowledge and understanding of children's learning and the role of play. They represent an equally diverse range of disciplines and educational philosophies and together they have strongly influenced modern nursery education. Some theorists have been misinterpreted. Some theories have been accepted in part. The general effect has been the popular belief that 'in a suitable environment the child is bound to select those experiences which will best further his development. The educational initiative must therefore rest with the child' (Tizard, 1976). Tizard goes on to examine other possible reasons for the current emphasis on free play. As well as being influenced by developmental psychology, some people have an intrinsic belief in the importance of individual autonomy, creativity and self-motivation, especially in the carefree pre-school years.

Learning through play and exploration requires a particular kind of nursery environment in which a huge range of materials and equipment must be provided to meet the learning needs of each individual child at any particular moment. Stressing individuality and creativity reduces the value placed on adult-initiated and adult-participating play and on rule-bound games and activities. As we shall see, these statements are based on observations within the nursery environment.

Observational studies

The application of ethological methods to the study of naturally occurring behaviour in young children has stimulated a number of studies using direct observational techniques to examine the nursery environment more closely.

Tizard *et al.* (1976a) found that children's play in the nursery was at a rather low level of complexity. Games were brief and simple with activities rarely lasting for more than five minutes. The authors argued that the free-play setting, which allows for child-initiated learning, also militates against a long attention span by providing such a great range of activities, lack of staff encouragement to persist and the distractions posed by large numbers of other children doing different things.

Sylva *et al.* (1980) reported similar findings from their observations in nursery schools and classes and playgroups. They suggested that the ethos of providing materials with little adult direction resulted in their observations, especially in nursery classes, of less social activity, more time spent alone and a high frequency of wandering about unoccupied.

Relatively few researchers have directly observed children with special needs in integrated settings to discover the level of their play. Chazan *et al.* (1980) confirmed that free play was the most common regime in the units which they studied. They were interested in three types of activity:

1. Child-directed activities where the child was free to choose what he or she did.
2. Activities suggested to the child by an adult which were partially or wholly supervised by an adult.
3. Adult-directed activities in which the child had to participate.

It was found, that for 15 of the 20 children with special needs observed, category (1) activities were dominant, an average of 75 per cent of the time being spent in this way. There were two cases of children who had no activity of the category (3) type.

Clark *et al.* (1977) observed children with a range of special needs in ordinary pre-school units and also observed matched control children. During free play activities the control children as a group were found to spend more time on imaginative play than children with special needs. In contrast, children with special needs as a group spent more time listening to and watching other children and engaged in non-specific activities.

A more detailed and structured observational schedule was used to observe 17 children with special needs in a range of pre-school units in the West Midlands (Clark, 1982; Robson, 1985; see Appendix 1 for the manual used). Again, matched control children in the same units were also observed. The social interaction aspects of this study will be considered in the next chapter. Of more interest here are the findings related to the activities of the children. The activities of the children with special needs were very similar to those of the control children. The control children as a group, however, were significantly more likely to spend time in book and story activities than children with special needs. Conversely, children with special needs spend significantly more time looking at and listening to others and waiting around. One child, who was described as withdrawn, spent 60 per cent of his time looking at others and not actively involved himself.

In what seemed to be a very busy environment, a surprisingly large proportion of time was spent by both groups either unoccupied or involved in routine nursery tasks. The 14 categories of activity were divided into two groups. The nine active categories in which children were involved in learning/play situations included fine and gross perceptual–motor activity, imaginative play, book/story activity, music and dance and conversing. The second group comprised five categories of inactivity and nursery routine including looking, listening and waiting, helping to tidy up and fetch equipment, toilet/washing, snacks and non-specific activity. It was noted that for some children, especially those recently admitted, some of the activities in the second group might be learning situations but, for most of the children observed, these activities were repetitive and routine. In some pre-school units snack time continues to be an opportunity for group discussion and learning but in most of those observed it was found to lack real stimulation.

Twenty-six of the 34 children observed spent at least 25 per cent of their time either unoccupied or engaged in routine tasks. Five children with special needs and two control children spent 50 per cent or more of their time in this way. Indeed, the withdrawn child already mentioned was unoccupied or routinely engaged for 76 per cent of the observation sessions. It is likely that for some children these percentages would be even higher, since many of the observations of gross physical activity (an active category) were of aimless movement around the nursery or playground.

THE NEED FOR SOME STRUCTURE

It is not advocated that free play should be abandoned in favour of a totally structured, adult-directed regime. Free play does have advantages for children in the nursery:

1. Children learn spontaneously through actively exploring aspects of their environment which interest them.
2. Children learn spontaneously from other children through observation and interactive play, a theme which will be developed in the next chapter.
3. Some children who live in restrictive home environments need time and space to play freely.
4. Young children have relatively short attention spans and require free play between concentrated activities.

The research reported above suggests, however, that too strong an emphasis on free play can be disadvantageous. Direct observation of individual children reveals a high percentage of time spent flitting and cruising from one activity to another. Some studies report that children may opt to spend much of their time in outdoor activities, thereby avoiding the more challenging 'educational' activities indoors (Tizard *et al.*, 1976b; Robson, 1985). Children with special needs have been shown to be capable of free play but may require adult guidance in order to get an activity underway.

If adults in traditional nurseries see themselves as organisers rather than teachers or even facilitators, then children are deprived of opportunities to learn from adults. As Tizard (1976) stresses,

> If the child spends his days in a closed, child-centred world, in which the main activity of the adults is to watch over him and provide him with play materials, how can he learn about the adult world? And if the adults don't engage in activity with or beside him, how can he acquire the skills and knowledge he needs?

It is, therefore, advocated that adults in the nursery should reappraise their modes of interaction with the children in their charge. It is not suggested that play should be turned into work.

Indeed, the debate about the relative importance of play and work in the nursery is purely semantic, since no meaningful distinction can be made in educational terms between the two concepts in relation to pre-school activities. Children can work very hard at their play. Staff must be encouraged to overcome the belief that adult involvement in play is taboo. They should be able to interact actively with children at all levels of play, thereby encouraging sustained participation and concentration and the development of more complex patterns of play. As well as contributing directly to the children's learning and cognitive development, the staff will be encouraging children to relate to each other and will be learning much more about the children as individuals, this being a crucial aspect of ongoing assessment and planning.

All learning, social development and emotional well-being in the nursery hinge on successful communication. Many children with special needs lack appropriate communication skills and staff may not be equipped to identify this problem and remedy the situation. Children who cannot interact appropriately may not develop social bonds with other children and staff. In other words, they may not be able to become socially integrated and it follows that they will not be able to participate fully in the learning environment of the nursery. The next chapter is, therefore, devoted to language and interaction in the nursery. The argument in favour of increased structure will be developed further and guidelines provided for staff to help them to interact more effectively with their children.

4

Language, interaction and social integration

In the last chapter I examined the aims and objectives of nursery education, the learning mechanisms of young children and their play and activities within the nursery. Throughout the chapter, frequent reference was made to social interaction and relationships in the nursery between staff and children and between children. This is because life in the nursery unit, as in all social groupings, revolves around language and communication. The child entering the nursery is introduced to a whole new social experience. From a language environment dominated by parents and a few friends and neighbours, the child goes into an environment where he or she must now learn to interact with numerous peers and strange adults. Moreover, he or she must become secure and confident enough in this noisy, initially frightening place to explore, to learn and to develop as a person.

It is, perhaps, amazing that most children do quickly adapt and become integrated into this new setting, within a few weeks forming attachments to particular members of staff and friendships with groups of peers. For some children, however, particularly those with special needs, this initiation into the nursery environment may be less successful. For a wide range of reasons, children may have poor language and communication skills and be unable to make and maintain contact with others. Social isolation inevitably follows and, with it, reduced opportunities for shared activities and learning. Ironically, poor language skills and withdrawn behaviour result in reduced interactions with staff and peers, thereby further ensuring that communication skills will not be stimulated.

Language and communication skills are, therefore, central to the social and functional integration of children with special needs. As Lindsay and Desforges (1986) point out, ultimately integration must be measured in terms of the actual interaction between the special children and their peers and teachers. We must be concerned with the nature and level of interactions, and the means whereby they are promoted.

In this chapter, the nature of children's communication problems will be considered. Observational studies of children in the nursery, particularly focusing on children with special needs, can reveal a great deal about how children cope with communication failure. The material is a valuable source of information to help staff identify problem areas and improve their own level of interaction with children. On the basis of information from this field of research, ways of helping children to become socially integrated and overcome emotional barriers to learning will be considered, from highly structured, instructional programmes to more subtle forms of adult intervention and management of the social environment. Further information is contained in another book in the present series which deals specifically with speech and language difficulties (Webster and McConnell, 1987).

CHILDREN WITH COMMUNICATION PROBLEMS

Children may experience difficulties in communicating for a variety of reasons, some of which will be briefly mentioned here.

1. Speech defects

Ingram (1965) suggested a classification of speech defects in childhood, which included disorders of speech sound production with demonstrable dysfunction due to neurological and local abnormalities. The former included upper and lower motor neurone lesions and nuclear agenesis. Local abnormalities referred to the jaws, teeth, tongue, lips, palate and pharynx, the most common problems being hare lip and cleft palate. These latter defects can be detected and generally repaired at an early age but some children still enter nursery with the defects unrepaired. Children with speech defects may be able to communicate but the quality of their speech may make them reluctant to attempt dialogue. Even after successful repair there may remain lack of confidence and a tendency to withdraw.

2. Language disorders

Language disorders are much more difficult to diagnose and define. Ingram (1965) offered the term 'specific developmental speech disorders' in which the speech abnormality is not attributable to disease or environmental factors. This would include receptive and expressive aphasia or dysphasia, congenital auditory imperception and central deafness (Mittler, 1970).

3. *Delayed language development*

Much more common in the nursery unit are delayed language and immature speech. The child is functioning at a language level several months below his or her chronological age. There are many possible reasons for this delay, including unsatisfactory home environment (Mittler, 1970), mild learning difficulties (de Villiers and de Villiers, 1979) and varying degrees of psychiatric disturbance and autism (Kanner, 1957; Cunningham and Dixon, 1961).

4. *Hearing loss*

Profoundly deaf children are likely to be detected at an early age. Partial or intermittent deafness may not be detected for many years, although there is now much greater awareness of the role of partial hearing loss in causing or contributing to language difficulties.

5. *Withdrawal*

The extremely withdrawn child, who is more than 'just shy', may have no speech and language disorders or even delayed development but cannot or will not interact fully in the nursery.

6. *Within the range of normality*

Not all children participate to the same degree in any nursery or classroom. Willes (1981), in a study of nursery and reception class children, found that teachers typically regard as satisfactory classes in which only some children offer replies, making only intermittent efforts to identify those who rarely participate. These quiet children are not necessarily withdrawn or in any way disturbed but require additional encouragement to participate.

7. *Disorders of conversation*

Children who fall into any of the above categories of communication difficulty might exhibit disorders of conversation. McTear (1985) discusses some of the characteristics of the communication of young children who have conversation disorders. They may find it difficult to initiate dialogue because they lack attention-getting skills. They may lack understanding of socially acceptable speech and appear impolite by making improper requests. Responses may be inappropriate and unrelated to preceding initiations, in extreme cases being echolalic, thus disrupting the flow of dialogue.

The surveys discussed in Chapter 2 all pointed to communication problems being the largest category of special need reported in ordinary pre-school units (Clark *et al.*, 1977, 1982; Chazan *et al.*, 1980). Many children were referred as having speech and language difficulties and many more were identified as having other special needs in addition to communication problems. Indeed, all of the seven types of communication problem were represented among the children in ordinary nurseries.

PERSPECTIVES OF LANGUAGE RESEARCH

Linguists have traditionally been interested in syntax and semantics, grammar and pragmatics, morphemes and phonemes. Language and grammar were studied in isolation from social interactions and context. The acquisition of language owed more to innate mechanisms, such as Chomsky's language acquisition device, than to environmental factors. As a result, during the past 20 years, linguists have solved the problem of analysis and the communication of data by developing extensive generative grammars (Coulthard and Brazil, 1981). As Tough (1973a) complained, we know what language is like but what does it do?

Dissatisfaction with this approach to language research, whereby meaningful behaviour is reduced to artificial ideal-typical structures (Stubbs, 1981), led to a growing interest in the study of the functions of language and the analysis of discourse (Brown and Yule, 1983; Coulthard and Montgomery, 1981; Stubbs, 1983). Discourse analysts were, however, slow to turn their attention to the pre-school child. This may have been due to mistaken beliefs that young children do not possess discourse skills and so do not hold meaningful, mature conversations, beliefs strongly influenced by Piaget's theories of egocentrism (Ervin-Tripp and Mitchell-Kernan, 1977).

A second reason might have been the lack of suitable methods for data collection. The observer paradox most certainly applies, related to the difficulties of observing how people speak when they are not being observed (Labov, 1972; Romaine, 1984). Pre-school researchers have attempted to record interaction by means of time-sampled observation schedules (Sylva *et al.*, 1980), handwritten narratives of conversation (Umiker-Sebeok, 1979) and directional microphones suspended from the nursery ceiling, which were found to be insensitive to the speech of individuals and over-sensitive to background noise. The advent of the radio microphone offered considerable potential in the study of communication in natural settings and began to be used with the pre-school child (Hughes *et al.*, 1979; Tizard and Hughes, 1984; Wells, 1985). With a radio microphone attached to a child, dialogue can be recorded while the child moves freely around the nursery, indoors and outdoors, without the close proximity of an observer. Transcription of tapes does, however, require some information about context and the non-verbal communications that are taking place (Todd, 1981; Gosling, 1981; Brown and Yule, 1983) and some researchers have attempted to evaluate the effect of observer presence during recording (Bernal *et al.*, 1971; Johnson and Bolstad, 1975).

Radio microphones were used by the present author to study the interactions of children with special needs in ordinary nursery units and in a special nursery for children with language problems. The findings of this study are highly relevant to the issues being discussed in this chapter and will be presented in some detail. As well as highlighting the nature of dialogue in the nurseries, the discussion will show that the use of radio microphone recordings can provide a wealth of information, which can be of great benefit to staff in inservice training as an aid to personal development and improved communication skills with children.

STUDY OF COMMUNICATION IN THE INTEGRATED NURSERY

The details of the research methodology are explained elsewhere (Clark *et al.*, 1982; Robson, 1985) and will only be outlined briefly here.

The language of ten 4-year-old children in ordinary pre-school units in Birmingham was recorded using radio microphones attached to target children. Five children had speech and/or language difficulties which had been assessed by a speech therapist. They attended three nursery schools, a nursery class and a day nursery. Each child was matched with another child in the same unit whose language development was felt to lie within the normal range. Target and control children were recorded simultaneously during two 90-minute sessions. Recordings were made during free play time when the children were allowed to choose from a large number of activities, both indoors and outdoors. Lunchtime was also included in each recording.

A research worker observed each child during recordings in order to note background information which would help to provide the context for the dialogue during transcription. Children wore radio microphones and transmitters concealed within butcher-style aprons. Up to 12 other children wore similar aprons so that target children would not feel that they were being singled out.

Immediately following the recording sessions, transcripts were made from the tapes. The dialogue between the target child and peers and adults was then analysed using Blank's cognitively based system of language assessment. Initiations and responses were analysed according to four levels of complexity, from basic matching perception, in which language is directly related to observable actions and objects, to abstract reasoning about perception. Responses were also coded according to their adequacy. Initiations were categorised as obliges (questions) or comments. Further information about this system of analysis will be given in Chapter 6 and full details are contained in Blank and Franklin (1980).

Adult to child initiations

Questioning

The majority of initiations from adults to children were questions rather than comments (an average of 87 per cent of initiations were questions, range 70–100 per cent). Approximately half of the questions were in the simple two choice category, in which the child only had to answer 'yes' or 'no' or choose from alternatives already given in the question, e.g. 'red' or 'blue', thereby giving no indication of whether the question had been understood. Children with language problems gave inadequate or ambiguous responses to 90 per cent of these adult questions. Many of these responses were accepted by the adults, who seemed unaware that the children might not have understood anything of the dialogue which had taken place. Able children frequently ignored simple two-choice questions from adults.

Complexity of adult language

Although there was a wide difference in the linguistic skills of the two groups of children, there was very little difference in the level of complexity of adults' questions and commands to children with and without language difficulties. Adult questions used simple, concrete concepts (levels I and II) and rarely used more complex structures.

There was a difference in the complexity of language used in adult comments directed to the two groups. Comments to the language-disabled children remained simple (level I and II), whereas almost half of the comments to the non-handicapped children were at levels III and IV.

Questions with multiple levels of complexity

Many questions were analysed at more than one level of complexity since, although the question may contain complex elements at levels III and IV, the child may only be required to grasp a simple level I component of the question in order to respond adequately. A total of 218 questions at levels III and IV were initiated by adults to children. Of these, more than half (57.5 per cent) contained simple level I components. On many occasions, therefore, staff may believe that children are handling complex, abstract concepts when in fact they are responding to only a small part of the question, perhaps not understanding more of what was said. For example, an adult said to one child, 'Why don't you <u>choose a colour</u> you'd like to paint the grass with and <u>bring it</u> here.' This statement contains complex language at level IV but the child need only understand the simple level I components (underlined) in order to respond.

Time for response

It can be difficult for staff in a large nursery to spend time with individual children, especially if a child is slow to respond. Consequently, adults often asked questions of children but gave no time to respond before moving away, going on to the next question or providing the answer. This adds to the frustration of a child with language problems who cannot successfully keep up with such a pace of conversation and who will give up trying.

Strategies of children with communication problems

Transcripts and recordings increased staff awareness of the strategies that a child with communication problems can adopt in order to cope with adult initiations and so avoid detection of his weaknesses. These would include:

1. Two-choice questions. Children may take advantage of two-choice initiations in order to give an acceptable answer. For example, in the following excerpt, the child may not have understood the meaning of 'few' or 'enough' but he appears to be participating in a meaningful dialogue:

    Adult: What do you want, Andrew? Do you want one sausage or two?
    Child: One.
    Adult: A lot of chips or a few chips?
    Child: A few chips.

Adult: Will that be enough or do you want more?
Child: Enough.

2. Minimum level of complexity. Children may ignore the more complex aspects and respond only to a simple component embedded in a question.
3. Cue dependence. Some children were strongly dependent on situational cues and context, sometimes being able to answer questions about objects and actions present before them, possibly without understanding the language used.
4. Imitation. In routine nursery situations, a child may imitate the responses of his peers in the hope that he will be correct, but lack of understanding can be revealed by a change in the adult's language. For example, a teacher had asked children round the lunch table if they would like one cracker or two. When she came to the target child with severe language difficulties, she asked him if he would like a cracker with cheese or without cheese. He said 'one'. He had imitated the replies of his peers in the hope that this might be appropriate.
5. Ambiguous reply. One child was found to grunt ('eh') when he knew he was expected to reply but was confused. Adults then interpreted this grunt as 'yes' or 'no' and the child happily accepted this interpretation.
6. No response. If a question is too complex, a child might say nothing and wait until the adult simplifies the question. In the following excerpt, Andrew had been painting pictures.

Adult: Would you like to have a go at another one or would you like to draw a picture for me up there? [*points to blackboard*]
Andrew: [*looks, does not reply*]
Adult: Would you like to draw a picture?
Andrew: Yeh.

7. Child-directed conversation. Most of the children in the study attempted to change the direction of the conversation if they could not cope. The child would suddenly make a comment which was irrelevant to the topic being discussed. If the adult then pursued this new line of conversation, the child had successfully avoided revealing his lack of understanding.
8. Frustrations of children with communication problems. The frustrations of children can be clearly seen by examining transcripts of dialogue. Sometimes the microphone picks up words which are not heard by the adults in the nursery, as in the following excerpt. Andrew has just completed a picture of his father, complete with beard.

Andrew:	Look!
Adult:	Are you finished, Andrew? [*comes to look*]
Andrew:	Yes, look.
Adult:	Let's have a look.
Andrew:	That's my pic ...
Adult:	[*interrupts*] That's nice. What's that?
Andrew:	That's a ... [*unclear*]
Adult:	Mm?
Andrew:	That's eye.
Adult:	Who's that?
Andrew:	He's got a beard on.
Adult:	[*does not understand*] What are you going to put on him now?
Andrew:	He's got a beard on. There. [*points*]
Adult:	[*does not understand*] What's that? [*points to beard*]
Andrew:	That's ...
Adult:	[*interrupts*] Oh, I know who that is, don't I?
Andrew:	Yes.
Adult:	Well done, that's daddy's beard!
Andrew:	Yes.

Child to adult initiations

Questions and comments

Whereas the majority of initiations from adults to children were questions, half of the initiations from children to adults were comments. Children generally made fewer initiations to adults than vice versa. A very withdrawn boy who had recently undergone a cleft palate repair made only three approaches to staff. A girl who was almost an elective mute in the nursery made no approaches to adults during either of the two sessions. She did, however, receive 269 initiations from staff, including 95 questions at level I and 83 at level II, to all of which she gave no response! She did respond adequately to four abstract questions requiring reasoning and relatively complex linguistic skills. It was suggested to staff that they reappraise their interaction strategy with this child since they were clearly reinforcing her mutism with extensive adult attention.

Complexity of initiations

Although the two groups of children differed in their language skills, all the children studied used simple, concrete concepts in most of their questions to adults. Comments by non-handicapped children were, however, more complex than comments made by language-disabled children.

Adequacy of adult responses

Only half of the questions and comments directed to adults by children with communication problems received adequate responses. On the occasions when adults did not respond adequately, they either ignored the child's initiation or requested the child to repeat or clarify what he said. Children with good communication skills were more likely to receive adequate responses to their initiations to staff. It is very important that the child with language difficulties receives as much encouragement as possible. The child must put a great deal of effort into formulating an initiation and into attracting attention. He or she will find it very difficult to repeat the initiation and perhaps impossible to clarify it. A 50 per cent inadequacy rate of adult responses would, therefore, seem detrimental to these children.

Adult repetition of child's initiation

Some adults habitually repeated what children said. For example, the following interchange took place in a nursery school:

Child: I've got new shoes on today.
Adult: You've got new shoes on, have you?
Child: Yes.

The child with communication problems cannot cope with this response since he does not know what to say next; he has not been helped in any way to maintain the dialogue. Some teachers and nursery nurses are aware that they use this strategy to end conversations with children if they are busy, but the teacher who engaged in it most frequently, out of habit, was unaware of its negative effect until reading several transcripts.

Child–child interaction

Questions and comments

Children with good language ability received more initiations from peers than did children with communication problems. While adult-initiated dialogue usually took the form of questions and demands, peer-initiated dialogue often took the form of comment. Most of the target children made as many initiations as they received.

Complexity of initiations

Peers seemed to take account of other children's levels of comprehension when initiating dialogue. Questions to children with communication problems were all simple, whereas 19 per cent of questions to more able children were complex and required more advanced skills. Comments from peers were generally more complex, to children with and without communication problems.

Adequacy of children's responses

Children with no language problems successfully responded to most of the initiations by peers. As expected, children with communication problems gave many more inadequate responses, but an interesting point was noted. Although comments initiated by peers to children with communication problems were generally at a higher level of complexity than questions, the target children responded more successfully to comments than to questions. In other words, the children responded more successfully to comments at level II than to questions at level I.

Peer stimulation

The frequency and general nature of child–child dialogue has been discussed. With the exception of the elective mute, all the children in the study engaged in dialogue with their peers. The content of their interactions highlighted the role of peers in stimulating language development. Full details of the various forms of peer stimulation are contained in 'Encouraging dialogue in pre-school units: the role of the Pink Pamfer' (Robson, 1983) and will be summarised briefly here.

1. Learning through imitation: learning of routine nursery language as well as non-routine language and the acquisition of new linguistic concepts.
2. Direct teaching. Children were observed to help each other pronounce words and to correct errors of pronounciation. Peer perception of errors was not generally detrimental to children with difficulties. Children would laugh and make fun of others who made uncharacteristic errors. They were much more tolerant of those with severe communication problems and rarely made negative comments. The following excerpts illustrate the child as teacher, or perhaps as speech therapist!

Peer:	Look! Rupert the Bear!
Anthea:	No, Pink Panther.
Peer:	Pink Pamfer.
Anthea:	You can't say it. Pink Panther, 'ther' not 'fer' – you can't say it. Say ther, ther, ther.
Peer:	Pamfer.
Anthea:	No, not with your teeth. Ther, Ther.
Peer:	Panther. Said it – yes!

In this extract a child notices that Anthea has not pronounced a name adequately:

Anthea:	You know Assif? He goes to big school.
Peer:	Who is Assif?
Anthea:	He used to come here, you know Assif.
Peer:	You can't say *Ass* ... if. [*stresses first letters*]
Anthea:	*Ass* ... if!

3. Language practice. The social situation of the nursery unit offers numerous opportunities for children to initiate dialogue and to respond to others using constrained formal language as well as spontaneous, informal and even idiosyncratic forms of language. Some of the most complex language was produced during fantasy play and role taking. Sometimes the children spontaneously acted out their favourite stories, organising the 'set' for their play and allocating parts. Here, Jane directs the story of the Three Little Pigs.

Jane:	Let's play the three little pigs. You be the big bad wolf and I'll be the second pig.
Peer 1:	John can be the big bad wolf again.
Jane:	Come on. Want to help me with the house? [*Jane and three children construct a house from large bricks. Five minutes later*]
Jane:	Come on. You be the wolves over there. You go and be the wolves over there.
Peer 1:	No, no.
Jane:	You come in the house them.
Peer 1:	[*comes in the house. To the second peer outside*] You say 'little pig, little pig, let me come in'.
Peer 2:	I know that.
Jane:	Right. You be the wolf then [*to peer 2*] and you come right in the house [*to peer 1*].
Peer 2:	Little pig, little pig, let me come in!
Jane:	No, not by the hair of my chinny chin chin.

Peer 2:   Then I'll huff and I'll puff and i'll blow your house in.
[*puff, puff*] I'll blow your house out!
Peer 3:   It's all gone now!
Jane: [*to peer 3*] No, you're not the wolf! You're a big
pig ... er ... little pig. You go and stand over there.

More time was spent discussing roles and organising the
actors than actually playing the parts but the children were
totally engrossed and the dialogue flowed rapidly.
   Mealtimes could be the focus of animated dialogue, especially if adults were relaxed, informal and did not attempt to
dominate the conversations, intervening only to help particular children to communicate more effectively. The opposite
situation was also observed, in which adults talked only to
each other and the children were subdued and did not
converse. Unstructured activities out of doors were not found
to be conducive to good dialogue between children.

STUDY OF COMMUNICATION IN A SEGREGATED NURSERY

As part of the Birmingham study, similar recordings were made in a
special nursery class attached to a school for children with language
problems. Two of the nine children in the nursery class were
studied, Helen and Sean, both aged 4 years. The procedure for
recording and observing was the same as in the ordinary nurseries.
Of particular relevance here were the differences which were found
between the interactions of children in this unit and those of
children in the ordinary units, some of whom had equally severe
language problems.

Adult to child initiations

Helen and Sean received considerably more initiations from staff
than children in ordinary units. An overwhelming percentage of
these initiations were questions rather than comments, approximately 93 per cent for both children. Fortunately, a minority of these
questions were simple, two-choice alternatives. Sixty-three per cent
of questions to Helen and 73 per cent to Sean were flexible,
open-ended questions encouraging greater understanding of the
language used and giving the child more scope in response.
   The language directed towards Helen and Sean was more
complex and challenging than that directed to children with
language problems in ordinary nurseries. Indeed, the complexity of

comments initiated by adults to Helen was almost identical to the pattern of comments initiated to normal children in ordinary units.

Although questions and comments to Helen and Sean were relatively complex, they achieved a considerable degree of success in responding to them. With the exception of Sean's low level of success in dealing with comments, their success rate was considerably higher than that of children with language problems in ordinary units and was more comparable to the performance of children with no communication problems.

Child to adult initiations

Helen initiated more dialogue with adults than any other child studied. She made 83 initiations to adults, 77 per cent of which were comments. Both children tended to use simple concrete language in their questions but slightly more complex language in their initiating comments.

Children with communication problems in ordinary units received adequate adult responses to only half of their initiations. Adults responded much more adequately to Helen and Sean. They received satisfactory answers to between 79 and 90 per cent of their questions to adults, while Helen received a higher percentage of adequate adult replies to comments (84 per cent) than any other child studied.

Reasons for superior adult–child interactions

Helen and Sean had very severe language problems, to the extent that they would not be understood at all by a listener unfamiliar with their speech patterns, yet staff were able to engage them in 'normal' dialogue. The following conversation took place in the garden and, although Helen's speech was *very* unclear, she understood what was being said to her and could formulate adequate responses. Two children are building a pretend fire.

Helen: Karen thinks that on fire.
Peer: Karen, come quick. It on fire.
Helen: It isn't! It isn't on fire.
Adult: I think he's playing a game. He's pretending it is. What would you do if it was?
Helen: We would call the police.
Adult: Call the police. Who else would you call?
Helen: A ambulance.
Adult: An ambulance. Who else?
Helen: A fire engine.

Adult: That's right. The fire engine. You'd have to call the fire brigade wouldn't you? And they would come rushing here with their big engine and lots of water and then what would they do?
Helen: Spray it all out.
Adult: Spray it all out, wouldn't they? Put water on the fire.

This transcript can be compared with the frustrations of Andrew trying to discuss his picture of his father which were described earlier. The excellent staff:child ratio (around 1:3) and the whole ethos of the special nursery class allowed the staff to develop and demonstrate skills which would not have been feasible in the ordinary units within their available resources. These benefits included:

1. Time to listen and to wait for a response.
2. Knowledge of speech patterns of individual children.
3. Knowledge of language ability of individual children, aided by close liaison and daily contact with speech therapists.
4. Structured activities: each child followed a structured programme for part of each day, devised by the teacher and speech therapist. The materials used were all readily available in ordinary nurseries but were more carefully selected and monitored in the special unit.
5. 'Unstructured' activities: much of the free play time, fantasy play and role taking was, in fact, structured by the staff and they frequently played an active part with the children.

Child–child interaction

The volume and nature of peer interaction in ordinary units has been discussed as well as the role of peers in stimulating dialogue and language development. Peer interactions involved children with and without communication problems. By comparison, there was virtually no child–child dialogue in the special nursery class. During three hours of recording, mostly during free play activities, Helen initiated only seven obliges and eight comments to peers. Sean asked four questions and made no comments. Similarly, peers initiated dialogue with Helen on 22 occasions (17 obliges and five comments) and only asked two questions of Sean.

STUDIES OF SOCIAL INTEGRATION

The Birmingham studies in integrated and segregated nursery settings indicate the wealth of data that can be generated and the value of such research for suggesting ways of improving practice and enhancing the success of integration. It must be said, however, that very little research of this nature has been carried out. As Sebba (1981) stated:

> Despite the apparent popularity of the ethological approach to the study of child behaviour adopted by Blurton Jones (1972) and many others, there have been relatively few applications of this approach to the study of handicapped children in integrated groups.

The following studies all deal with some aspect of the integration of pre-school children with special needs, but it will be seen that they are not all directly relevant to the pre-school settings with which we are concerned.

Two studies have looked at social interactions and choice of playmates in integrated settings and reported no differences between handicapped and non-handicapped children. Peterson and Haralick (1977) concluded that true social integration was in evidence, but generalisation must be limited by the fact that handicapped children outnumbered non-handicapped children in the nursery by 8 to 5. Similarly, Sebba (1981) found that there were no significant differences between overall patterns of interaction for handicapped and non-handicapped children and that they showed no preference in choice of playmates for 'their own kind' or differences in their interactions with adults. Again, however, developmentally delayed children outnumbered normal children by a ratio of 6 to 4. Sebba does, in fact, list 10 other reservations which limit generalisability of these findings.

Chazan *et al.* (1980) observed 20 children with a range of handicapping conditions in ordinary nurseries. Their main finding was that the numbers of adult contacts which any one child received were controlled by the child's behaviour.

> If the child was restless and aggressive he was the focus of considerable adult-initiated contact and was seen by adults as demanding … . Withdrawn children were not given sufficient adult-initiated help and encouragement simply because they did not know how to attract attention successfully.
>
> (p. 210)

This is similar to the findings of the time sampled observation study carried out by Clark *et al.* (1982). There was no significant difference between the two groups of children (those with and without special needs) in the amount of individual adult attention received but there were some interesting observations related to special needs. Three children who had been identified by staff as being withdrawn and having communication problems were observed to spend *no* time alone with an adult. On the other hand, three over-reactive boys who took little part in group activities all received much more individual attention from adults than did other children. Indeed, one boy spent as much as 25 per cent of his time alone with staff.

Kaplan-Sanoff (1978) found that handicapped children in mainstream pre-school provision made more overall gains in general areas of development than did similar children in segregated provision. Down's Syndrome children have also been found to make significant gains in developmental quotient and language skills when attending ordinary nursery units when this was combined with intensive stimulation and maternal involvement (Ludlow and Allen, 1979).

Sinson and Wetherick (1981) also examined the integration of children with Down's Syndrome and were less optimistic about its success. The children in their study had been attending a special nursery from a very early age. They were judged to be socially competent and could feed and toilet themselves with little help. They were given some experience of attending ordinary playgroups from the age of 3. The first child was felt to have settled well in playgroup and to the casual observer and the staff she appeared to be socially acceptable and little different from the other 20 children in the group. Close continuous observation over two hours revealed a rather different picture. She had no verbal interaction with other children and spent only 18 minutes in constructive play. Eighty minutes were spent in inappropriate and non-constructive play in situations she coped well with in the special nursery. She engaged in aggressive and attention-seeking behaviour which had not been a feature of her interactions in the special nursery and she had involved staff in 33 minutes of one-to-one interaction, the extent of which they had been unaware of.

Observations of other Down's Syndrome children in this integrated setting confirmed that they too became social isolates in terms of interaction with peers. Because they conform to group norms and cause little trouble to the staff, their isolation can go unnoticed. The ordinary children in the playgroups were observed to make great efforts to be friendly and initiate interaction during the child's first days of attendance but they gave up eventually because of lack of response. This was due to the Down's Syndrome children's lack of ability to establish contact and mutual gaze, which are essential components of social interchange. The authors question the value of this integration experience for the children with special needs and suggest that the 'possibility may exist of identifying the deficit demonstrated by untypical mutual gaze behaviour in the DS children and correcting it by training'.

In a discussion of a programme in Australia aimed at integrating pre-school children who evidenced delayed development, Ashby (1978) reached similar conclusions. Placing a handicapped child in an ordinary nursery without supportive specific tutoring leads to rejection of the child and reversion of development. 'Minimal support from a non-professional helped with professional consultant, however, promotes socialisation and competence.'

THE NEED FOR SOME STRUCTURE

This examination of communication and social integration brings us to the same conclusion as was reached at the end of the last chapter, which considered cognitive development, play and nursery activities. Learning in pre-school education takes place within the social setting of the nursery, in which communication and interaction skills play an important part. Children learn from adults and also from each other. Segregated special provision has been seen to provide a stimulating learning environment in terms of teaching and adult input but can be a barren social environment, with little or no opportunity for peer stimulation at the level experienced by children in ordinary nurseries.

It would be naive, however, to expect social integration to occur simply because a child with special needs is placed in an ordinary nursery. Many children have been shown to have great difficulty in communicating and establishing contact with others, both adults and peers. Staff in ordinary nurseries may have good intentions and a desire to help children with special needs to integrate but they lack the skills and resources which are found in specialised teaching staff. As a result, they may fail to identify a child's needs or, having identified a need, they may use the wrong strategies to remedy the situation.

Failure to communicate and interact socially is one of the greatest barriers to learning that is experienced by children with special needs. Staff can do so much to alleviate these difficulties and there is no reason why they themselves should not begin to function at the level of competence demonstrated by special nursery staff, given adequate knowledge, information about their children and appropriate resources. The next chapter will consider ways in which staff, advisers and planners can help break down barriers to learning and bring some of the strengths of special education into the ordinary nursery.

5

Breaking down barriers to learning

Examination of children's development and activities in the nursery has led to the conclusion that structure is necessary in pre-school education, particularly if our concern is that children with special needs should be integrated as fully as possible into the nursery curriculum. This chapter will consider how the nursery environment can be planned and structured to break down barriers to learning and enable all children to achieve their maximum potential in terms of cognitive, social and emotional development. While the focus will be on the 20 per cent of children identified by the Warnock Report as having special needs, it is likely that many of the other 80 per cent of 'normal' children in the nursery will have specific individual needs at any given time and so all children can benefit from the suggestions which will be made regarding structure.

It is necessary first of all to define 'structure', since this is a highly emotive term that has stimulated a great deal of debate and attracted unfortunate connotations.

STRUCTURE DEFINED

Structure is frequently associated with formality, rigidity and an authoritarian regime. It is against the principles of freedom, self-determination and the right of the pre-school child to experience fun and enjoyment. The term arouses visions of Victorian discipline and a formal academic curriculum. We can react with horror and condemnation to extreme examples of rigorous academic instruction, such as is found in Japanese kindergartens. The Ministry of Education in Japan has warned that the formal teaching of *kanji* (Japanese characters) and numbers to pre-schoolers may be stifling their spontaneity, while the emerging role of Japanese kindergartens as preparatory schools is leading to 'exam nerves at kindergarten' (Casassus, 1987). American educationists are debating whether young children benefit from academic instruction and Lillian Katz warned recently that children can become 'burnt out' by the age of 5 if early cramming at school turns pupils off learning (Hackett, 1987).

Of course, it will not be argued here that pre-school children should be subjected to a structured academic curriculum in which activities are controlled and totally directed by adults, leaving no room for spontaneity and freedom of choice. Rather, structure will be seen as something that planners, teachers and nursery nurses do but to which children should be oblivious. To structure is 'to organise' and 'to construct a framework for' (MacDonald, 1972). Adults can structure without imposing a rigid regime. They can be directive without physically controlling and pushing a child into an activity. The child should experience his environment as pleasurable, stimulating, challenging and secure.

Observation of children in the nursery has highlighted some of the dangers of an unstructured environment. In a setting which appears to be a hive of industry, children can actually spend a large proportion of their time flitting from one activity to another. With so many activities to choose from and no adult encouragement to concentrate on a task for any length of time, the child's attention span is short and distractions are many. Children with special needs may find it difficult to start an activity. They may also find it difficult to interact with their peers and make contact with adults. Left to their own devices, they can become socially isolated. In this environment, staff may not be aware of each child's needs and the child can indeed disguise his or her problems, especially if he or she can conform to group behaviour and avoid attracting staff attention. These factors have led some writers to advocate a high degree of structure in the nursery, especially where children with special needs are involved (e.g. Blank, 1972; Tizard, 1976; Chazan, 1978; Widerstrom, 1983).

Flexibility and an awareness of the needs of individual children are called for. Some will require more direction than others. Needs and priorities will change and so objectives and methods will have to be reviewed and adapted. Clark (1983a) advocates that children with special needs should be allowed opportunities to learn spontaneously and 'only if this does not succeed would it seem appropriate to resort to the "elaborate" teaching of skills'.

In this chapter, some of the barriers to learning will be considered. Each child's needs will be special to that individual and so it is impossible to make general statements about how to structure the environment to overcome barriers to learning and to promote successful integration for all children with special needs; the reader will be asked to consider various options. Whether the adult in the nursery adopts the role of observer, teacher, facilitator or participant will depend on assessment of the needs of individual children and how these can best be met within the constraints of the nursery environment and the needs of the group as a whole.

BARRIERS TO LEARNING

The development of pre-school provision in this country has created an artificial distinction between child care and education. Few would disagree that both should be involved in any pre-school provision and there is a growing awareness of the importance of good quality care as a prerequisite of good education since 'it is only from this sound secure framework of social relationships that young children gain confidence in themselves and build up positive attitudes to their own learning' (Watt, 1987). The main components of quality child care have been identified as familiarity with a consistent group of adults and children, responsiveness on the part of adults who interact with children on the basis of their value as individuals, and attachment resulting from the development of emotional bonds between adult and child and within peer groups (Tizard, 1986). A strong emotional bond between child and adult enhances mutual satisfaction in shared activities and learning (Morgenstern *et al.*, 1966).

Introducing the child into the nursery

The implications of this line of thought for the integration of pre-school children with special needs is obvious. Before the child can begin to explore and learn within the nursery environment, emotional security and social acceptance by adults and other children must be experienced. Therefore, the initial entry and introduction of the child into the nursery group requires careful planning. Staff are familiar with the fact that all children must cope with the transition from home to school, with separation from parents and with the strangeness of their new environment. Some handicapped children may have particularly strong attachments to home and parents brought about by the extra attention and care which their needs require. They may have been over-protected and sheltered from outside experiences or isolated from social contact because of illness. As we have seen, the nature of their presenting needs may affect their ability to make contact and interact with others.

The onus is on the nursery staff to make this transition for the child with special needs as easy and as successful as possible. First of all, teachers, as well as nursery nurses, must adopt the role of carers and feel comfortable in this role. As Winnicott (1964) pointed out, 'every child at a nursery school is at certain moments and in certain ways an infant needing mothering (and fathering)', but this aspect of a teacher's role has received very low priority. It must be borne in mind that a 3-year-old with learning difficulties, delayed development or behavioural problems may be functioning at the level of a 2-year-old and have the emotional needs of a 2-year-old. Staff should, therefore, recognise that social and emotional needs take precedence over educational needs, at least in the early days.

Blatchford *et al.* (1982) provide many useful suggestions for handling the first transition from home into nursery. Some recent guidelines have been published which give practical advice to staff when a child with special needs is about the enter the nursery. The entry of a girl with Down's Syndrome has been described (Mortimer, 1986) and the special requirements of hearing impaired children have been outlined (Webster and Ellwood, 1985). The following summary of general points may be helpful for children with a range of special needs.

1. Contact with parents. Parents are experts on their own children. Not only will they be willing to provide a family history, they will also be happy to answer questions about the day-to-day needs and likes and dislikes of their child.
2. Information seeking. The nursery staff should attempt to gather as much information as possible about the child. If they are fortunate, a record of needs will be available, which will provide details of assessments by medical personnel and an educational psychologist as well as a written statement by the child's parents. In addition, staff should obtain information from any other professional person who has had involvement with the child. This might include an educational home visitor, Portage worker, speech therapist, social worker, health visitor or physiotherapist. Useful information can also be obtained from specialist organisations and associations with interest in specific needs such as spina bifida, epilepsy, muscular dystrophy, cerebral palsy, etc.
3. Home visits. The nursery staff who will be most involved with the child should make at least one home visit before enrolment. This will allow staff to see the child behaving naturally in his or her own environment and to learn about handling the child by observing him or her interacting with parents. The child will also gain security from seeing a friendly relationship develop between family and nursery staff.

4. Nursery visits. It is now common practice for children to visit the nursery once or twice with their parents before enrolling. Preparation for entry may have to be extended for children with special needs. Webster and Ellwood (1985) suggest that the hearing-impaired child should visit the nursery with a parent one afternoon a week for the half-term before entry. This helps the child to become familiar with the nursery setting and also allows staff to observe the child and determine any immediate changes which will have to be made to meet initial needs. The nursery can be flexible in deciding how long the parent should stay with the child once regular attendance has begun.

5. Enabling strategies. This refers to any obvious strategies or points of practice that must be taken into account to make the environment as welcoming as possible for the child and to enable him or her to function without being unnecessarily handicapped. For example, attempts should be made to remove any physical barriers which would impede a physically disabled child. If the child is able to attend to his own needs in the toilet, it would be extremely detrimental for him to have to depend on others for assistance simply because the toilets are unsuitable. Communication with a hearing-impaired child should take into account the acoustics and the child's position in relation to the speaker.

6. Maintaining home/nursery links. Some children may not be able to tell their parents what they have been doing at nursery and it would be useful if they could regularly take home items from the nursery, such as handiwork, photographs or pamphlets describing any nursery outings, so that parents can build up a scrapbook at home and discuss activities with their children. Similarly, parents might like to keep a brief diary of domestic events and weekend outings which staff can then use in conversation with the child.

Some of these preparation strategies will be standard practice for any child entering the nursery. Preparation for the child with special needs will, however, need to be more structured, with detailed early planning and close attention to small details that can make life much happier for the child. Careful introduction of the child into the nursery is only the first step in breaking down barriers to learning. The remainder of this chapter will examine more long-term strategies for helping the child to achieve social and functional integration.

THE PHYSICAL ENVIRONMENT

The important features of the physical environment of the nursery which affect the integration of children with special needs relate to the space available, the layout and organisation of that space and the equipment and facilities provided.

Layout and use of space

Early studies of space in the nursery concentrated on crowding variables and the effects of changing social and spatial density (e.g. Hutt and Vaizay, 1966; McGrew, P.L., 1970; McGrew, W.C., 1972; Loo, 1972). A lack of rigorous methodology led to few significant results and generally added confusion to the scene. A more thorough and extensive study by Smith and Connolly (1980) varied the spatial density per child in the nursery by altering the space and amount of equipment available. They found that the main effects were on choices of activity. Not surprisingly, in a larger space there was more running, chasing and vigorous use of apparatus. A smaller space meant more physical contacts between children but no significant change in social or aggressive behaviour. When more equipment was available, children played in smaller groups or alone, with less sharing of equipment. On the basis of this research, it could be suggested that a child with special needs would feel more secure in a smaller space but this is probably an over-simplification. The use of space in the nursery is obviously a factor which staff must consider within their own situation. The important point to stress is the need for flexibility and a willingness to experiment with use of space and layout of equipment. Too often a nursery is organised in a particular way because that is the way it has always been organised. A friend's child came out of nursery school one day after six months of attendance, very excited and bursting to tell his mother that 'the water moved today!' Unable to elicit any further information, the mother made enquiries at the nursery next day to learn that the water trough had been moved from one part of the nursery to another! It is sad that such an insignificant change in an otherwise static environment should create such interest and excitement.

A related physical feature of the nursery over which staff may have little control is the layout of the space in terms of overall size and number of rooms. Older traditional nursery schools and classes are likely to have been housed in standard sized classrooms. More modern purpose-built nurseries may be of a large, open-plan design. In one nursery it may be necessary or desirable to locate children with special needs in a small resource room for part of the nursery day. In another nursery, it may be necessary or desirable to locate children with special needs permanently within a large open-plan room. Whatever the necessity or choice, these options have different implications for the children and require different responses from the staff. Clearly, a 60 place nursery with three rooms and a 60 place open-plan nursery present very different environments for a child. Again, little research has been carried out into the effects of physical location.

There is some evidence that an open-plan setting, with its larger social grouping, makes it more difficult for children to get to know each other well and limits sustained imaginative play (Smith, 1976; Tizard *et al.*, 1976b). Lindsay and Dale (1982) report the findings of a study by Albutt (1980), which lend some support to this conclusion. Albutt studied 'ordinary' and 'special' children in two integrated nurseries. Unit B was largely oriented to free play techniques, with the special children located in a large open-plan room along with the other children in the nursery. Unit C involved the special children in a considerable amount of teacher-directed activity along with other children in a small room separated from the main nursery by a corridor and doors. All the children spent part of the day in the main nursery. Ordinary children in Unit C spent 31 per cent of the time initiating verbal interaction with special children, compared with only 1 per cent of the time for ordinary children in Unit B. Lindsay and Desforges (1986) also worked with children in Units B and C. In addition, Unit A had a separate room for special needs children separated from the main nursery by a corridor and steps and plans were underway to knock down a wall and create a more open environment. The authors expressed surprise, however, that their own observations and the findings of Albutt indicated that:

> merely having a more open setting is not, in itself, facilitating. Staff in Units A and C, well aware of the constraints of their buildings, engineered integration: children would go from one setting to another as a result of teacher initiation. In Unit B it was easy to be misled by the physical presence of the special children in the nursery and to overestimate their social and functional integration.

Standard equipment

It is not intended here to list all the items of equipment that a nursery should provide. This has been well documented and discussed elsewhere (e.g. Jeffree *et al.*, 1977; Curtis, 1986). Indeed, nurseries tend to be very well equipped and the problem can be one of too much, rather than too little. Several points regarding the provision of equipment should be borne in mind.

1. Value. Staff should reflect on the purpose of each piece of equipment and activity on offer. It is not suggested that every toy and game should have implicit educational significance but staff should be aware of its relevance.
2. Redundancy. An item may have been widely and usefully employed by the children when it was first introduced but eventually interest wanes or the pattern of play becomes stereotyped. Removal of equipment for short periods can renew its value when it is reintroduced.
3. Monitoring. The value and use made of equipment can be monitored making time-sampled observations. For example, an observer might decide to focus on use of the sand tray. During one hour of free play activity, observations can be made at 30-second intervals, noting which children are involved, what they are doing, whether they are interacting and so on. The effect of the presence of an adult involved at the sand tray on participation by children can be observed. Such structured observation can produce surprising results which might not be predicted from casual observation.
4. Accessibility. As much equipment as possible must be accessible to children with special needs. Safety is an obvious priority. Again, only close observation of the child will reveal the extent of his or her capabilities and the areas where he or she needs assistance. Means can be devised of helping a child to gain some value and pleasure from most of the equipment and activities in the nursery.

Specialised equipment

Some children will require special equipment and furniture to aid mobility, sitting position, use of the toilet and washing facilities, access to stored equipment, sensory perception and so on. An area of carpeting might improve acoustics for a hearing-impaired child. The possibilities are as numerous as the individual needs of the children and again individual assessment is necessary. Advice can be obtained from parents, physiotherapists, psychologists, special school staff and other specialist organisations. Skilled parents, sometimes of other children in the nursery, have been known to construct special furniture and equipment to help a particular child. Some provisions should be made in advance of the child entering the nursery, others will only become apparent with experience of the child's needs. Appendix 2 provides a list of resources and addresses of organisations which supply or adapt play equipment for children with special needs.

KNOW YOUR CHILD

Barriers to learning and integration can only be broken down if these barriers have been identified. We have already discussed the need to discover as much as possible about a child and his or her needs before admission to the nursery. Staff will continue to learn about the child through their growing relationship and observations of the child in the nursery. In a small nursery class, there may only be two members of staff, but in a large nursery school, especially of open-plan design, one or two members of staff must be given particular responsibility for a child with special needs and the child must know who they are. An additional member of staff may have been appointed to improve the staff:children ratio on the admission of a child with special needs but it need not be this person who becomes most involved with the child. The extra member of staff may be given general duties in the nursery in order to free another teacher or nursery nurse to work with the child.

Continuous assessment and monitoring of a child's progress are crucial and will be discussed fully in the next chapter.

STRUCTURED PROGRAMMES

As has been discussed, most children with special needs can engage in play activities, even though they may need more encouragement and direction from staff to do so. It is advocated that children with special needs should be involved as much as possible in the normal nursery curriculum. For some children, however, a highly struc-tured programme might be necessary and beneficial, as either a short-term measure or a longer term teaching strategy.

Some children may enter nursery with a specific problem that is overwhelming and affecting all areas of functioning. Parents may identify a particular problem which they are finding to be a barrier to their child's progress or which is affecting their relationship with their child, and they need urgent assistance to overcome this difficulty. Behaviour problems may suddenly emerge in a pre-viously settled child and disrupt his or her general ability to function in the nursery or present a danger to other children. All of these presenting problems require immediate intervention to identify the cause of the problem and help the child to overcome the difficulty.

Other children will benefit from participation in a structured programme over a longer period of time. For example, hearing impaired children have very specific needs relating to communica-tion skills and will require to spend some time in a one-to-one or small group situation with a teacher. Structured programmes have been devised to encourage language and cognitive development in pre-school children who have communication problems and delayed development. Nursery staff may not wish to introduce fully such programmes into their curriculum but they should be aware of what is available. They can then turn to a suitable programme if they feel that a child or group of children might benefit or if they are looking for ideas and guidance in a particular area.

Behaviour problems

Behaviour modification techniques have been widely applied within ordinary and special education but mainly at junior and secondary levels rather than in the pre-school. In an extensive review of studies in behaviour modification in British educational settings, Merritt (1981) mentions only one nursery study in detail, by Wheldall and Wheldall (1980), who attempted to improve children's eating behaviour. Nursery practitioners may feel that behavioural programmes are alien to pre-school practice but in fact many of their interactions with children and the learning situations which they set up incorporate behavioural principles. A behavioural programme simply makes the goals and contingencies more explicit.

A behavioural programme is highly structured and designed to meet the specific needs of the individual child. Certain features are common to all programmes. If the aim of the programme is to eliminate an undesirable behaviour, these features would include observing the child to ascertain the frequency and nature of the behaviour (establishing a baseline) and selecting reinforcements to discourage that behaviour and encourage more appropriate behaviour. Reinforcement must be given immediately so that the child makes the connection between actions and the consequences of actions. Because of this, a member of staff must be prepared to focus continuously on the child for the duration of the programme. Reinforcements should be largely positive by the rewarding of acceptable behaviour. For many children, praise and attention from an adult may in itself be sufficient reward to ensure success. Other children may require some more tangible rewards, such as tokens, stars, access to favourite activities and privileges. In extreme cases of highly undesirable behaviour a 'time out' procedure might be used – removal from the situation in which the behaviour occurred, perhaps by sitting on a chair or going to another room. A case study reported by Newman and Pitchford (1988) will illustrate the application of some behavioural techniques.

Stephen was referred by nursery school staff to the school psychological service because of aggressive behaviour. He was aggressive towards other children, especially in turn-taking or sharing situations, and aggressive to staff who tried to correct him. Stephen attended morning and afternoon sessions and engaged in around four fights daily. Observation of Stephen revealed six broad categories of behaviour difficulties: non-compliance, being frequently off his seat, running around the nursery, attention-seeking behaviours, needing one-to-one attention to settle to an activity and aggressive behaviour towards peers.

The programme contained the following procedures:

1. Compliance training. This took the form of the game 'Simon Says'. The nursery nurse played this game for two minutes at the beginning of morning and afternoon sessions, initially on a one-to-one basis and later with Stephen in a small group. This procedure required Stephen to obey a rapid succession of simple instructions and so encouraged compliance.
2. Positively phrased rules. Four rules were to be taught to Stephen which were incompatible with his undesirable behaviour: share, walk, sit and play and be friendly.
3. Script for introducing rules. Young children need to be shown examples of good and bad behaviour in relation to each of the above rules. Scripts were provided to help the nursery staff to discuss each concept with Stephen.
4. Condition statements and praise statements. Condition statements precede a behaviour that is to be encouraged while praise statements follow the behaviour. For example, the adult might say 'Stephen, I'll be very pleased if you sit and finish this puzzle'. If the child complies, the adult should say 'good boy, you finished it, I'm very pleased'.
5. Partial praise statements. When Stephen was engaged in appropriate behaviours, staff gained his attention and praised him.
6. Management of hazardous and non-hazardous behaviour problems. Three strategies were used to correct undesirable behaviour. Minor behaviour problems were ignored while children nearby were praised for appropriate behaviour. More serious problems were corrected by a positively phrased reprimand, reminding Stephen of the rule. Dangerous behaviours were controlled by separating Stephen from his friends for five minutes (time out), then rewarding good behaviour when he returned.
7. Record keeping. Successes were recorded on a star chart.

Parents were involved throughout the programme. Over the course of 12 weeks, fights decreased from around 20 per week to one a week. Aggression towards staff ceased altogether and

Stephen began to seek praise by drawing attention to his good behaviour.

This study has been presented in some detail because it highlights the dramatic effect that a relatively simple programme can have on a child's behaviour. Behaviour change was brought about almost entirely by a nursery nurse, with only limited involvement of the psychologist who set up the programme and monitored progress.

Behavioural programmes can have a powerful effect and there are many pitfalls that could lead to undesirable changes in behaviour. For this reason, a behaviour modification programme should only be drawn up in consultation between nursery staff and an educational psychologist who is trained in this technique. If staff in a particular nursery find that behavioural techniques work well with some of their children they may become skilled in this area, but involvement of the psychologist should always be sought.

The Portage Project

The Portage scheme, discussed in detail in Chapter 2, is used mainly by parents at home, under the supervision of a home teacher. Some children may enter the nursery having been involved with a Portage programme for many months. Frequently nursery entrance means the end of Portage for a child because the home teacher is withdrawn, mainly because the nursery staff take over the teaching role with the child and family. There may be no need for Portage to stop altogether, especially if the child and family have been benefitting from involvement in the programme. The nursery could become the focus of parental support and guidance. A member of staff with suitable experience and training could meet parents on a regular basis to discuss goals and progress. The parents then feel that they still have some part to play in their child's education and they are also encouraged to come into the nursery and get to know the staff.

Portage has been introduced into some nurseries as a programme for staff to use but the success of this has yet to be determined. Staff may certainly wish to consult sections of the Portage Guide for ideas to help them in their work with children, particularly in the areas of self-help, language and motor and cognitive skills.

Anson House Project

The Anson House Project at the Hester Adrian Centre in Manchester produced several research papers on various topics relating to the integration of severely mentally handicapped pre-school children.

Sebba (1980) describes a system for assessment and intervention aimed particularly at teaching behavioural principles to parents, but the book contains many practical ideas for nursery staff. The Bayley Scales of Infant Development (Bayley, 1969) are described in detail. The Bayley scales assess behaviour from birth to 2½ years and so are applicable for older children with learning difficulties who are functioning at a lower mental age. Two scales are employed, a mental scale and a motor scale.

Details are given for full sensory assessment, including sight, hearing, tactile, taste and smell. A self-help skills questionnaire was devised with items relating to feeding, toiletting and dressing. Detailed assessment procedures then lead to the selection of goals for teaching and of rewards for learning. The procedure is similar to that of the Portage scheme but the target behaviours and tasks are at a more basic level of development and rewards are much more explicit.

The system was devised for profoundly retarded multiply handicapped children but the principles and procedures apply equally to more able children and, therefore, this could prove to be a useful resource for nursery staff.

Language programmes

Marion Blank is one of the strongest supporters of the view that children with poor communication skills cannot be helped in a group situation but require one-to-one, structured teaching with an adult. In the group situation it is too easy for the child to conform and disguise his or her lack of comprehension, using some of the strategies described in Chapter 4 (Blank and Solomon, 1969). Blank's programme for nursery teachers, called *Two Speak to Learn*, outlines some of the principles for individual work with children (Blank, 1976). She advocates:

1. The imposition of a wider range of cognitive demands.
2. The sequential development of a theme in which the child is asked questions that arise logically from experience.
3. The careful presentation of materials.
4. The selection of materials on the basis of verifiability.
5. The encouragement of physical activity on the part of the child to reduce stress.
6. The pacing of the lessons so that difficult ideas are presented first, before the onset of fatigue.

The child learns through meaningful dialogue with the teacher but the dialogue is structured in such a way that only topics relating to the physical world and logical relationships are discussed. Thoughts, feelings and the actions of other people are not permitted since the validity of the child's statements cannot be verified by the teacher. As Lomax (1979) points out, this is the main feature that distinguishes Blank's programme from that suggested by Tough (1973a, b, 1977). Blank suggests that children should receive short, regular sessions of one-to-one teaching within this framework. It should also be stressed that Blank's concepts of language and interaction have considerable relevance for helping staff to improve their communication skills with children generally.

A rather different approach is used in the Inter-Reactive Learning Method (INREAL) devised by Weiss (1981). This programme aims to help teachers become better listeners and so emphasises child initiation and direction rather than teacher direction. The teacher's role is to be silent, to observe, to understand and to listen.

Some language programmes have been devised for use with groups of children. These include the Peabody Language Development Kits (Dunn *et al.*, 1968), the Bereiter and Engelmann programme (1966) and the Talk Reform programme devised by Gahagan and Gahagan (1970). These have not been extensively used in British pre-school education, largely because staff feel that they are too rigid and dismiss the importance of initiative and spontaneity in the child. It could also be argued that children's language needs are so individual and specific that group teaching cannot succeed.

The NFER My World Programme

This programme was devised by Curtis and Hill (1978) to meet the needs of socially handicapped children. More specifically, it aims to help the child who has weak self-image, poor language skills, delayed cognitive development and low levels of concentration. Activities centre on nine themes, which are used in sequence, beginning with the child and his or her family and extending to wider concepts, such as animals, transport and seasons. The programme has been found to be successful in achieving many of its aims (Curtis and Blatchford, 1981; Dye, 1984).

Summary

A few words of caution are necessary. The majority of children in the nursery do not require the high degree of structure described in these various approaches. If staff identify a child who would benefit from some individual stimulation, then the materials and method should be carefully chosen. Teachers should feel free to use a part of a programme that is felt to be appropriate and to modify and adapt the teaching method to suit the child. These programmes provide useful resources and ideas if used selectively and appropriately. As Lomax (1979) found, 'sometimes approaches resting on entirely different theoretical foundations are used together in one pre-school curriculum'.

ADULT AS FACILITATOR AND PARTICIPANT

We have examined ways in which staff in the nursery can facilitate integrated learning by carefully planning a child's entry into the nursery, structuring the physical environment and providing specific individual programmes when necessary. We will now consider the role of the adult as facilitator in a broader sense in relation to the activities of the children in free play and their social interactions with each other and with staff.

Management of adult–child interaction

During the past decade there has been growing awareness of the need for planned interaction in the nursery, requiring more active involvement of staff to facilitate communicative competence and dialogue. Indeed, staff behaviour may be the single most important factor in determining the nature of children's interactions and the degree of social integration experienced by children with special needs (Guralnick, 1976; Barnes, 1979; Dewhirst, 1985).

Katz (1985) outlined four basic principles underlying practice in the areas of language acquisition and communication competence:

1. The development of communicative competence is facilitated by interaction.
2. Interaction requires content (see also Blank, 1985).
3. Interaction is facilitated when the content is ecologically valid to the participants.
4. Interpersonal as well as communicative competence is facilitated when children experience others' responses to them as contingent upon their own.

Katz goes on to outline various practices that facilitate and inhibit communication. Many such guidelines were presented in the previous chapters on language, interaction and social integration. Staff must be alert to opportunities for encouraging dialogue, even when doing routine chores such as washing up and clearing away, especially when they are with only one or two children (Payne,

1985). The mealtime situation is ideal for developing communication and staff in attendance should be alert to opportunities for encouraging passive children to contribute to conversation. This does not mean adult-dominated dialogue but rather requires considerable sensitivity to the needs and skills of the children in the group. Extensive research by Wood and his colleagues, much of it with hearing-impaired children, has shown that not only does teacher style in dialogue influence spontaneity and contributions from children, but also teachers can alter their style of interaction along a continuum of power and control (Wood *et al.*, 1980; Wood and Wood, 1983, 1984). The study of children's interactions in other situations, most notably in the home, can shed further light on the processes which facilitate and inhibit dialogue in young children (MacLure and French, 1981; Tizard and Hughes, 1984; Wells, 1985).

Management of child–child interaction

The management of adult–child interaction involves greater understanding of the importance and influence of dialogue style and a clearer awareness of the factors affecting individual children's responsiveness. Few nursery practitioners would dispute the fact that adults must play some part in communication with children in order to foster language development and social relationships, even though their approaches and degree of involvement will differ.

The management of child–child interaction is likely to be met with greater suspicion and negative reaction. Certainly, most children are capable of forming friendships and negotiating social status and power without obvious adult intervention. The introduction of children with special needs into the ordinary nursery will, however, require staff to consider ways in which social integration can be encouraged and this will inevitably require them to become more actively involved in child–child relationships and the social networks of the nursery. The communication problems which affect many children with special needs and their potential for social isolation have already been discussed. It has been recognised for some time that simply placing children with special needs into groups of more able children does not necessarily lead to cross-group peer imitation or interaction (Cooke *et al.*, 1977; Strain and Shores, 1977), and this has led behaviourists to consider ways in which a structured, behavioural approach could be applied to stimulate interaction and learning. This stance was summed up by Strain *et al.* (1977), who stated that:

> It would seem that integrating children who display good social skills with isolate youngsters could be employed to enhance the latter's

social behaviour development. It should be emphasised, however, that the mere integration of children with divergent social repertoires would probably not result in positive social development. Rather, careful instruction and programming of peers seem to be required.

An obvious means of encouraging child–child interaction would be to provide materials and structure activities which bring children together in associative and co-operative play. Katz (1985) points to the usefulness of developing a project over time, involving children in joint construction and role playing. She gives the example of children developing a hospital ward environment and using it as the basis for imaginative play. A member of staff can actively attempt to integrate children with special needs into such groups by encouragement and by taking a part in role play.

A more highly structured approach may be necessary where children present more severe problems. A number of studies have been carried out recently, attempting to teach children to interact with less able peers. Odom *et al.* (1985) raise the important issue of whether 'pre-school aged children have adequate social repertoires for independently generating a variety of successful social initiations when interacting with a peer who is consistently unresponsive', and they suggest that some teacher prompting will always be required, even at a minimal level. Nevertheless, some researchers report considerable success in this area of peer tutoring (Greenwood *et al.*, 1987). Odom *et al.* (1985) paired able children with children who had behaviour problems. The tutors were asked to share, share request, assist, show affection and compliment their partners and their partners did indeed increase their social responsiveness. Interesting spillover effects have been reported, whereby untrained peers will observe the 'tutor' and copy his behaviour, so increasing their interactions with the less able child (James and Egel, 1986). Similarly, it has been found that the social behaviours of handicapped children may increase as a result of observing their more able peers (Strain *et al.*, 1976).

Goldstein and Wickstrom (1986) found that two peer tutors trained by staff successfully raised the level of interaction of three peers who had behaviour disorders and development delay, and that the improvements continued after training had stopped. The importance of the perceived status of models has been pointed out (Sasso and Rude, 1987). Kirby and Toler (1970) selected a 5-year-old withdrawn child to distribute sweets to others before free play and found that peer interactions greatly increased. Sainato *et al.* (1986) developed this research further by giving withdrawn children managerial roles in the nursery in which they directed their peers in highly enjoyable tasks. The selected child was given a manager badge and organised and delegated activities, such as feeding the guinea pig, collecting milk money, taking lunch count and ringing the bell for clearing up. A child was in this managerial position for 10 days after which he or she was publicly praised for his or her efforts and another child was chosen. The researchers found that when three socially withdrawn children were placed in managerial roles they:

> substantially increased the frequency of their social interactions during free play time, were the recipients of many more positive and significantly fewer negative social bids from their peers, were rated more positively by their peers and were selected more frequently as best friends by their peers.

Follow-up suggested that there was some maintenance of these effects. This was attributed to the increased visibility of the child, the leadership role and possibly the fact that the child already had social skills but lacked performance skill. Practice at performance encouraged the child to put social skills into action.

A behavioural approach to the management of child–child interactions might, therefore, be a useful tool for encouraging social integration of some children with special needs. An important factor that will influence the outcome of such an intervention is the child's level of cognitive functioning and his ability to perceive and make sense of the behaviour of his peers, in his role as either 'manager' or 'pupil'.

—6—

United responsibility: assessment, record keeping and professional support

The nursery practitioner, having read this far, might be dismayed by the wide range of new demands that will be imposed by the introduction of children with special needs into the ordinary nursery. The special needs of the children will be varied. Staff will be faced with problems which they have never before encountered. Some children will have obvious and previously identified needs. Others may manifest characteristics and behaviours that lead staff to suspect special needs which have so far not been identified. It will be clear from our focus on the child in the nursery that staff will require considerable imagination, ingenuity and flexibility as they seek ways of helping children with special needs to take maximum advantage of all that is offered within the full curriculum. In order to achieve maximum functional integration, greater emphasis must be placed on assessment of children's strengths and weaknesses, programme planning and record keeping than has been tradition-ally found in pre-school education, further extending the role of the nursery staff.

The nursery staff, however, are not alone in their responsibility for meeting the needs of the children, nor can they be expected to adopt new roles without extensive support and training. This section will, therefore, focus on the adult in the nursery, or more appropriately, on adult input to the nursery, since the theme of united responsibility will be developed.

This chapter will consider assessment and record keeping in relation to nursery staff and professional support agencies. It will be argued that assessment and monitoring of progress should be seen as the focus of multi-disciplinary teamwork and the basis for united responsibility for meeting the needs of individual children and of the nursery as a whole, bringing together parents, staff and support agencies.

The following chapter will examine more specifically the exten-ded role of the adults in the nursery by considering the skills required by nursery teachers and nursery nurses and the necessity of imparting these skills through initial and inservice training. Parental participation in nursery education has received considerable attention in recent years. The contribution made by parents has been very varied and generally dependent on the attitude of individual head teachers and staff members. The case will be argued for encouraging greater involvement of parents when there are children with special needs in the nursery, to the mutual benefit of all concerned.

THE NEED FOR ASSESSMENT AND RECORD KEEPING

> Any training programme will only be as good as the assessment of strengths and weaknesses on which it is based.
>
> Laing (1979)

In practice, assessment and record keeping are closely linked. The results of a particular assessment will determine the nature of the records to be kept. Conversely, the use of a particular record card within an LEA or an individual nursery unit will determine the range of assessment procedures to be carried out.

Until recently, record keeping was not considered to be a necessary function within nursery education. As recently as 1979, it was stated that:

> The keeping of written records is accepted in primary and secondary schools although it must be admitted that their quality, quantity and value varies from teacher to teacher. Additionally, there is written evidence of change over time in the form of the child's own written work. Many practitioners in the pre-school field, sensitive to the dangers and limitations of written records, are opposed to any form of record keeping.
>
> (Clark, 1979)

There are, indeed, dangers inherent in record keeping. Unstructured assessments are open to subjectivity on the part of the observer. Staff in different nursery units may use different criteria for assessing children and even staff within the same unit can make very different judgements about children. Someone consulting a record at a later date could misinterpret the information. There has been little consensus about what should be recorded and how it should be recorded. At a more fundamental level, many workers in the pre-school field have been reluctant to assess, record and possibly label a child at such an early age.

As a result, the literature on pre-school record keeping is very limited. A recent survey found, however, that there has been a considerable increase in the use of nursery records during the 1980s (Moore and Sylva, 1984). They attribute this new interest in record keeping partly to the publication of two manuals of pre-school assessment (NFER and Keele, to be discussed later) and a comprehensive review of tests for use with young children (Bate *et al.*, 1981), all of which provided more 'objectivity' in assessment. The trend towards the integration of children with special needs into ordinary nursery education and the requirements of the Education Act 1981 undoubtedly provided further stimulus for a more structured approach to assessment and record keeping.

Pre-school assessment procedures fall into two broad categories. First of all, developmental screening may be applied to all children in the nursery. This usually takes the form of checklists of behaviour and ability, along the lines of the NFER and Keele assessment guides, and provides a general record form. Screening in this way helps staff to develop and monitor the nursery curriculum and also identifies areas of special need. The second category of assessment would include more detailed and in-depth examination of individual children who are perceived as having special needs. Such assessment would be carried out by nursery staff and by specialists within education and health, depending on the nature of the child's needs.

Record keeping, therefore, serves several purposes, some of which are summarised below.

1. Evaluation of the curriculum. Screening identifies areas of the curriculum where aims and objectives are not being met.
2. Identification of special needs. Screening helps staff to identify children with special needs who may then need further assessment and individual attention.
3. Programme planning. Individual programmes for children with special needs must be regularly monitored and progress noted.
4. Communication. A number of people will be interested in a child's assessment, progress and nursery programme and these can only be communicated accurately through a written record. The most important channels of communication in this respect are with colleagues in the nursery, with parents and with other members of the professional support team.
5. Transition. When a child moves on to another nursery or into a reception class in school, some form of written record should be passed on, particularly if that child has special needs (for further discussion see Chapter 8).
6. Statement of special educational needs. The Education Act 1981 makes it possible for a statement of special educational needs to be drawn up for pre-school children with special needs. The

initial statement requires intensive assessment by education and health authorities and input from parents and is reviewed annually. Ongoing written records are essential if this process is to be meaningful.

IDENTIFICATION OF SPECIAL NEEDS

The nature and severity of a child's special needs determine the stage at which these can be identified. Pre-school identification falls into three broad categories, detailed below.

Identification at birth

Some handicapping conditions are obvious at birth. Indeed, advances in antenatal care and the more widespread availability of amniocentesis mean that some abnormalities in the baby can be detected before birth. Amniocentesis involves the removal of a small amount of the amniotic fluid that surrounds the foetus in the womb. Analysis of this sample can reveal the presence of spina bifida, Down's Syndrome and an increasing number of relatively rare blood disorders and brain abnormalities. At the present time, elective abortion of an abnormal foetus is available but some parents will choose to allow the pregnancy to continue, using the time up to the birth to find out more about the nature of their child's likely condition and preparing to cope with the demands which this will impose.

When special needs are detected at birth, the family can be offered assistance from a variety of sources. Counselling should be available immediately. The health visitor and general practitioner have a central rôle to play. Educational home visitors or social workers may make initial contact with the family in the first weeks, as described in Chapter 2. Support can be offered by voluntary organisations, many of them employing counselling officers and social workers. It must be stressed that each family will react in a unique way to the birth of a child with special needs and early intervention must be highly experienced and sensitive so that appropriate support is given at the correct time and in the most useful way.

Identification during the pre-nursery years

Special needs may become apparent during the first two or three years of a child's life, mainly because developmental milestones are not reached at the appropriate age. For example, a child who does not sit up at around 6 months and does not develop mobility in the following months may suffer from a physical disability such as cerebral palsy. The child who fails to develop language during the second year may have a hearing deficit or learning difficulties. Again, regular attention by health visitors and GPs will detect such problems at an early stage. The Education Act 1981 (Section 10.1) specifies that health authorities have a duty to take the following steps:

> 10.(1) If an Area or District Health Authority, in the course of exercising any of its functions in relation to a child who is under the age of five years, forms the opinion that he has, or probably has, special educational needs, the Authority shall –
>
> (a) inform his parents of its opinion and of its duty under this section; and
>
> (b) after giving the parent an opportunity to discuss that opinion with an officer of the Authority, bring it to the attention of the appropriate local education authority.

Section 10.2 requires the authority to inform the parents of the existence of a particular voluntary organisation that is likely to be able to give advice and assistance.

Identification during the nursery years

Children in the above two categories will enter the nursery having already been identified as having special needs, although the exact nature and consequences of these needs might not have been fully assessed. They may enter nursery as priority admissions. A third group of children will enter nursery in the usual way and their special needs will be identified during their time in nursery. Health authority staff still play an important role in assessing children at this stage, but nursery staff may be the first to suspect that a child has difficulties by means of direct observation and developmental screening.

DEVELOPMENTAL SCREENING

Two screening schedules have already been mentioned. The *Keele Pre-School Assessment Guide* (Tyler, 1980) looks at a child's level of performance in the areas of language, socialisation, cognition and physical skills. Scores are recorded on a circular chart, which provides a very good graphic profile of the child's strengths and weaknesses.

The NFER *Manual for Assessment in Nursery Education* (Bate and Smith, 1978) is a similar instrument which examines five areas of a child's development: social skills; talking and listening; manual and tool skills; thinking and doing; and physical skills.

A new developmental screening and monitoring tool entitled the *Schedule of Growing Skills* (Bellman and Cash, 1987) promises to be a useful instrument for medical practitioners and nursery staff. Nine fields of activity are assessed, giving a total of 180 behaviours in developmental sequence, but administration takes only 10–20 minutes. A book with the same title is also available.

The *Pre-School Behaviour Checklist* (McGuire and Richman, 1987) was devised to detect behavioural and emotional problems in young children aged 2–5 years. The checklist contains 22 items, requiring the observer to decide on the degree to which a particular behaviour is exhibited. The *Behaviour Assessment Battery* (Kiernan and Jones, 1982) is a useful book which provides a range of tests, questionnaires and checklists designed to assess cognitive and self-help skills.

All the screening schedules mentioned above are available for use by nursery staff. In their survey of under-fives record keeping in Great Britain, Moore and Sylva (1984) found that the Keele guide and NFER manual were the two most frequently used checklists and many LEAs and nurseries had devised their own checklists and records based on these two publications. As well as identifying children with special needs, checklists such as these were used by LEAs who wished to evaluate the work being done in their nurseries. Moore and Sylva found great variability in the nurseries, even within one LEA, and they argued that this accounted for the lack of any standard system of assessment and record keeping, stating that 'the predominance of "schools' own" systems means it will never be possible to suit everyone with a standard system, unless … it is bland and only meant to be a partial system in the first place.'

OBSERVATIONAL SKILLS

Screening procedures and behavioural checklists require the assessor to have detailed knowledge and information about the child being rated. Some of this knowledge will be acquired as the member of staff forms a relationship with that child on a day to day basis. As was argued in Chapter 3, however, it is easy to form the wrong impression of a child by casual observation. Feelings about the level of a child's involvement and integration in the nursery may be subjective and inaccurate. Nursery staff must be given time to observe individual children and they will be greatly aided in their observations if they have a structured schedule. This will help them to focus their attention on relevant behaviours and to be objective in their analysis. Direct observation will teach staff a great deal about the normal level of functioning of children in the nursery and will highlight the problems encountered by children with special needs.

The present author devised a manual for observation in pre-school units and this is contained in Appendix 1. The schedule incorporates 14 categories of activity, five categories of social location and an indication of the frequency and nature of a child's interactions with staff and other children. As explained in the manual, it is recommended that a complete observation should be made every 30 seconds and that a suitable observation period is 20 minutes, but obviously this can be altered to suit individual needs.

An observation schedule for use in nurseries was devised as part of the Oxford Pre-School Research Project and guidelines for training staff are available (see Holmes and McMahon, 1978; Sylva *et al.*, 1979, 1980).

FURTHER ASSESSMENT BY NURSERY STAFF

Having carried out observations in the nursery and used a screening instrument, nursery staff may have identified some children as having possible special needs. It may be necessary to examine more closely specific aspects of a child's development and there are many useful tools and guidelines available to assist nursery staff.

The *Pragmatic and Early Communication Profile* (Dewart and Summers, 1988) provides a descriptive and qualitative assessment of language from 9 months to 5 years of age. The focus is on how the child communicates in real situations rather than in a testing situation and allows parents to contribute information based on their knowledge of the child at home.

The *British Picture Vocabulary Scale* (Dunn *et al.*, 1982) and the *Sentence Comprehension Test* (Wheldall *et al.*, 1979; revised edition Wheldall, 1987) both provide information about a child's understanding of language.

Marion Blank's system for analysing dialogue was discussed in Chapter 4. As well as being a useful guide to study natural dialogue in the nursery, this system gave rise to the *Pre-School Language Assessment Instrument* (Blank *et al.*, 1978). This gives a profile of a child's language skills and qualitative information on the nature of the child's responses to questions of different levels of complexity. Four levels of complexity are represented, each by 15 questions. Examples of the type of questions at the four levels are given below.

Level I: matching perception

In order to respond to questions at level I, the child must demonstrate understanding of language that is closely related to perceptual information, generally actions and objects which can be observed. Level I demands include:

1. Simple labelling. (What is this called?)
2. Imitation of simple sentences. (Say 'the boy saw the car'.)
3. Carrying out simple instructions. (Touch your nose.)
4. Matching by scanning an array of objects.
5. Immediate recall. (What did you just see?)

Level II: selective analysis of perception

At this level, the child still attends to objects and actions that are present but focus is now on different aspects and characteristics of the material, such as shape, colour, size and weight. The following skills are included at level II:

1. Function of objects. (What do we do with scissors?)
2. Sentence completion. (Finish this: 'I like to eat some ... '.)
3. Identifying differences and similarities. (Shown a tricycle and a bicycle and asked 'How are these different?')
4. Scanning for an object defined by its function. (Find me something I can cut with.)
5. Describing a scene. (What is happening?)
6. Recalling details from a story presented orally.

Level III: reordering perception

The child is required to reorder his or her perceptual experiences since what is seen will not help response to level III questions. The following are examples of level III demands:

1. Following directions in sequence. (Touch hair, stand up, clap hands.)
2. Assuming a person's role. ('What did she say to the dog?')
3. Request for exclusion. (From an array select all the objects that are not clothes.)

4. Similarities between objects. (What is the same about scissors and a knife?)
5. Definitions of words. (What is a car?)
6. Continuing a story. (What did the boy do next?)
7. Telling a story from a sequence of pictures.

Level IV: reasoning about perception

Verbal formulations at level IV are the most complex and abstract. Tasks involve going beyond the salient features of objects to reasoning and problem solving and test demands at this level include:

1. Predicting the course of events. (What will happen if ... ?)
2. Justifying prediction. (Why will ... happen?)
3. Marking and justifying inferences. (How can we tell that ... ?)
4. Identifying causes of events. (Why did ... happen?)

Children are expected to have acquired all of these skills by the time they enter school but even the child with very severe difficulties in the nursery is likely to enjoy some success on this test by responding to some level I items. Because it is possible to use the same levels of complexity when analysing natural dialogue in the nursery, a child's profile on the test can be compared with ability in a non-test situation, often with interesting results.

Various structured programmes were discussed in the last chapter. For example, if Portage materials are available, staff may wish to assess a child using this scheme and plan a programme accordingly. Resources should include good, up-to-date reference books so that staff can learn more about particular special needs or indeed find information to help them decide whether a child manifests a suspected problem.

These are just some examples of the materials available to nursery staff who wish to assess children with suspected special needs. It must be stated, however, that responsibility for assessing special needs does not rest entirely with nursery staff: if a teacher has reached the stage of employing one or more of the above tests, it is likely that discussions about the child will already have taken place with a psychologist or other specialist. A teacher may feel more confident about whether a child should be referred for further assessment if some initial assessment has been carried out in the nursery.

ASSESSMENT BY SPECIALIST SUPPORT TEAM

One of the advantages of segregated nursery education for children with special needs is that a wide range of professional support is available, often based within the special school itself. Professional support for children with special needs in ordinary nurseries must be equally wide ranging and available. Nursery staff should be able to call upon psychologists, speech therapists, social workers, specialist teachers, health visitors, GPs and paediatricians, depending on the nature of the special needs presented by their children.

As will be discussed later, some of these advisers should be in regular contact with the nursery but others will be involved only when the need arises and a particular child requires attention. Each professional group has its own specialised tools and methods of assessment, but in communicating the results of their investigations to nursery staff, parents and others, it is important that they should use plain language, avoiding technical terms and professional jargon. This may seem an obvious point but it is worth stressing because writers often seem to forget to whom they are addressing their reports.

Nursery staff will be familiar with the names of some of the testing materials employed by other professional groups and it might be useful to summarise some of the more commonly used procedures in order to demystify the contents of the little cases and boxes that frequently accompany psychologists, speech therapists and others!

Intellectual ability

Intelligence tests generally provide an intelligence quotient (IQ), with the average IQ falling between 90 and 110. Many psychologists will not include the actual IQ in a report. They will describe the child's profile and ability to cope with particular problems, this being more meaningful than an IQ which could be misunderstood or misinterpreted.

The *Stanford–Binet Intelligence Scale (Form L–M)* (Terman and Merrill, 1960; Thorndike, 1972) can be used from around 2 years of age. A wide range of cognitive skills is examined, including vocabulary, understanding and use of language, memory, story telling, comprehension and reasoning ability. Matching, sorting and simple construction tasks are included as well as the copying of geometrical shapes.

The *British Ability Scales – Revised* (Elliot *et al.*, 1983) are similarly designed, with groups of tests at each age level from about 2½ years. Tests designed specifically for younger children include the *Merrill–Palmer Pre-School Performance Scale* (Stutsman, 1931) and the

Weschler Preschool and Primary Scale of Intelligence (Weschler, 1967), both of which provide measures of performance and verbal skills. Children with communication and hearing problems may need to be tested non-verbally. The *Leiter International Performance Scale Battery for Children* (Leiter, 1948) is a non-verbal performance battery in which instructions are mimed rather than spoken and the children respond by matching blocks to corresponding strips positioned on a wooden frame. The battery can be administered to children from the age of 2 years. Similarly, the *Snijders-Oomen Non-Verbal Intelligence Scale* (Snijders and Snijders-Oomen, 1976) can be used to assess hearing- and speech-impaired children from the age of 2½ years. Children with visual impairment may be assessed by means of the *Reynell–Zinkin Scales for Young Visually Handicapped Children* (Reynell and Zinkin, 1979). These scales assess social skills, motor ability, reactions to the environment, under-standing and use of language and communication skills.

Language skills

One of the most frequently used language assessment instruments is the *Reynell Developmental Language Scales: Second Revision* (Hunt-ley, 1985). The scales measure children's expressive language and verbal comprehension. Verbal comprehension scale 'A' includes ten sections moving from assessment of children's understanding of single words to their comprehension of complex instructions. Verbal comprehension scale 'B' is similar but requires only minimal eye-pointing responses, which makes possible the testing of withdrawn children and those with severe physical difficulties. Twenty-five activities are included in the expressive language scale, again arranged in developmental sequence from the language of a 1-year-old to around the 7 year level.

Two recently developed packages provide language assessment procedures and guidelines for therapy. The *Assessment and Therapy Programme for Dysfluent Children* (Rustin, 1987) involves parents in the assessment of their children's difficulties by means of an interview schedule. The follow-up programme gives guidelines for two weeks of intensive work in which parents are given tasks to complete with their children at home to consolidate the work of the speech therapist. Alternatively, the programme can be adapted to allow for weekly sessions over a longer period of time. This is an excellent example of the way in which parents can be usefully involved in their children's learning and this theme will be discussed in more detail later. The *Bristol Language Development Scales* (Gutfreund, 1988) examine both pragmatics (how a child uses language) and semantics (the meaning of a child's language), as well as how the child forms language. The scales were developed from the Bristol Language Development Research Programme, which studied the language of 128 pre-school children (see Wells, 1981, 1985).

The language tests discussed above all examine children's understanding and/or use of language. The speech therapist who wishes to study the actual sounds a child makes in speech might use the *Phonological Assessment of Child Speech (PACS)* (Grunwell, 1985) which involves obtaining a sample of a child's speech for analysis and development of a programme of therapy. In order to elicit the necessary sample of speech, Grunwell (1987) produced *PACS Pictures: Language Elicitation Materials*, a book of pictures designed to encourage the child to say particular words. Further information about language assessment procedures used by speech therapists is contained in Muller *et al.* (1981).

These, then, are some of the procedures that might be applied and mentioned in reports, particularly by psychologists and speech therapists. The list is not intended to be exhaustive and there are many more tests and programmes in current use. As already stated, professional reports should always be written in straightforward, non-technical language. Nursery staff should feel free to question aspects of a report relating to test results and it may be helpful if they could be shown the materials used and perhaps even be given a demonstration.

Discussion of assessment by the professional support team has concentrated so far on tests and structured interviews but, as with assessment by nursery staff, direct observation of children in their natural environment must be an important element of any pre-school assessment. Pre-school children can be extremely suspicious and reticent in the presence of strange adults and children with special needs are often the most difficult to assess because of the very nature of their problems. It is strongly proposed that all initial assessment, as far as possible, should be carried out in the child's home or nursery and not in an office or clinic that is strange to the child. Formal testing may still, however, produce highly uncharacteristic results and must be supplemented by observation of the child in the nursery and/or at home.

In a short study of 11 children, Robson (1985) compared natural dialogue with test performance, using Blank's language assessment procedures (described in previous chapters). Only four children showed a close match between their performance in the nursery and their performance in a test situation. For the remaining seven children, the test considerably underestimated their ability, as demonstrated by recordings made of their interactions in the nursery. This was attributed to lack of confidence in a formal test situation, particularly when children had communication problems.

It is often argued that the professional adviser's workload does not permit time for observation of children in the nursery. Professionals claim that it is something they would like to do but that it is a luxury which they cannot afford. This need not be the case. Observation has been shown to be a necessity, not a luxury, and it would be much more profitable and relevant for the assessor to spend an hour observing a child in the nursery than an hour trying to elicit responses from the child in a testing situation. The observer can use time in the nursery most constructively and efficiently by employing a structured observation schedule. The use of a radio microphone is highly recommended.

THE ROLE OF PARENTS IN ASSESSMENT

Parental participation will be discussed in detail in the next chapter but the role of parents must be stressed at this point in relation to assessment. Parents can be involved in the following ways:

1. Initial discussion. When special needs are suspected, parents can describe the child's general development and performance at home, in discussion with nursery staff and other professionals.
2. Specific observations. Parents might be asked to focus on specific behaviours and keep a written record over a period of days or weeks. For example, if a child is showing signs of extreme anxiety, parents could keep a record of these episodes, noting the circumstances in which they occur, the length and severity of the attacks and how the child was helped to overcome the anxiety. A pattern might be revealed, giving clues to the causes of the anxiety, perhaps separation from a parent or sibling or engaging in particular activities. If the nursery staff are finding difficulties with toilet training a child, the parents could keep a daily record of their successes and failures in this area. Parents can also communicate their specific observations by means of a structured interview which forms part of an assessment procedure, as described above.
3. Exchange of information. The communication of information should be a two-way process. Parents can provide valuable information and must also have access to the findings of assessment and observation by others. If parents have knowledge of test results, checklist profiles and their child's

individual programme they will be able to contribute more effectively to their child's learning and also monitor changes in behaviour which occur at home.

MINIMISING THE PAPERWORK

It has been advocated that records should be kept for all nursery children. The records of children with special needs will necessarily be more detailed and extensive and will need to be updated more frequently. As Gulliford (1983) suggests, there must be a framework for objective recording but there must also be space for diary records and anecdotal notes which might prove to be useful at a future date. Such recording and the unwieldy nature of piles of paper have, in the past, made the task time-consuming, undesirable and often ineffective. Gulliford goes on to suggest that the use of a computer for entering, storing and retrieving such information is likely to be of increasing benefit to schools. A strong case can, therefore, be made for the widespread introduction of the 'nursery micro', as indicated by Moore and Sylva (1984).

STATEMENT OF SPECIAL EDUCATIONAL NEEDS

An important part of the Education Act 1981 relates to the identification and assessment of children with special educational needs. Detailed guidelines and recommendations to assist LEAs to carry out procedures laid down by this legislation are found in DES/DHSS Circular 1/83 (DES/DHSS, 1983). It is the duty of each LEA to identify children with special needs, to carry out multi-disciplinary assessment, to make recommendations for meeting special needs and to maintain and review a statement of these needs and recommendations (this statement is referred to as a Record of Needs in Scotland).

> The Act's definition of Special Educational Needs applies to children under 5 who are likely to have a learning difficulty when over this age or whose learning difficulty would be likely to persist if special educational provision were not made for them.
> Circular 1/83 Sec. V.65 (DES/DHSS, 1983)

LEAs do not have a duty to make statements for children under statutory school age but they may carry out an assessment and make a statement for a pre-school child who is brought to their attention by parents or other interested parties. The actual nature of the assessment is left to individual authorities but, at the very least, it should include contributions from parents, a psychologist, a medical officer and, where relevant, a teacher. Hegarty (1987) discusses this legislation in some detail and only three important features relevant to pre-school education will be highlighted here.

1. This legislation emphasises the early identification of special needs and regular review of the statement to ensure that any changes in circumstances are taken into account without delay and that recommendations are altered accordingly.
2. The requirement that several disciplines and parents should contribute to a single written statement makes the process of assessment and review a focal point of united responsibility. This is summed up by the Scottish Education Department in their guidelines for the implementation of this legislation with regard to the under-fives:

> Education and social work authorities and health boards should develop existing links so as to establish and maintain effective channels of communication between them. They will wish to ensure that assessment arrangements are co-ordinated, delays minimised and stress on the family reduced as much as possible. Parents should be informed in the early stages .... All this calls for regular and systematic communication and co-operation between staff of the education authority and the health service, involving also social work departments, and voluntary agencies.
>
> Circular 10/83 (SED, 1983a)

3. Parents were seen to gain most advantage from the new procedures. As Hegarty (1987) remarks, based on Rutherford's (1986) appraisal of Recording in Scotland:

> Parents now had formal rights, specifically in respect of consultation. They obtained a copy of the document containing the professional assessment of their child. This strengthened their hand in dealing with the professionals who simultaneously became more accountable and more precise in what they said about children.

Useful guidelines to help parents write a parental profile and report on their child at home are contained in Wolfendale (1987) and in a Scottish Education Department guide (1983b).

NAMED PERSON

Parents are being given an increasingly prominent role in the decision-making processes regarding their young child with special needs. As we have seen, they are being brought into each of the stages of identification, assessment, programme planning and monitoring. Even if a statement is not made several professional agencies will have shown an interest in their child. If a statement is made, parents are being asked for the first time to contribute written evidence to their child's record and the full statement will be shown to them.

The benefits to parents are obvious and to be welcomed but at the same time the pressures on parents are increased. They must come to terms with their child's disability. They must learn about available provision and the role of each of the professionals who will be involved in assessment and in giving advice. They may have to undertake medical investigations themselves to try to determine the cause of their child's disability and the possible likelihood of future children being similarly affected. In addition to all of this, their time and energy may be entirely taken up with caring for their child on a day-to-day basis.

Parents may not understand the system. They will be given written guidelines but for some parents these will not be very meaningful and for all parents there will be many questions to be answered. The concept of a named person, as recommended by the Warnock Committee, is a very valuable one and a necessity for families such as have been discussed. The named person is basically a knowledgeable person who is in regular contact with the family, and has been variously described as a keyworker, facilitator and befriender. This person must be in a position to:

1. Get to know the child well.
2. Be readily accessible to the family to answer questions and give advice.
3. Act as a link between family and professionals, explaining the roles and responsibilities of each professional agency to parents.
4. Ensure that assessments are carried out without unnecessary delays, that statements are drawn up efficiently and that reviews of statements take place at the recommended times.

This may seem an impossible burden to place on any professional who already has a heavy workload but, in practice, the main function of the named person will be to determine the families' needs at any given time and to direct them to the appropriate agency. The Warnock Report (DES, 1978) recommends that the health visitor should most frequently be the named person for children under 5 years. Certainly, health visitors have a great deal of contact with families, especially in the early days, and this may indeed be appropriate. Alternatives should also be considered, however, since health visitors have a wide remit and may not be able to become involved as named person for every family in their area with a handicapped pre-school child. The following hypothetical case studies will help to illustrate not only the wide range of professional involvement with a child but also the factors governing choice of the most suitable named person.

James, aged 10 months

James has spina bifida which was diagnosed at birth.

> Presently involved:
> Parents
> Educational psychologist
> Physiotherapist
> Health visitor
> Counselling officer (Association for Spina Bifida and Hydrocephalus)
> Paediatrician

Choice of named person: The counselling officer from ASBAH would be ideal. This person has detailed knowledge of the child's medical condition and its implications and is in regular contact with the family. Some parents may prefer a named person from a voluntary agency rather than a local authority or health board employee since the former is seen to be 'neutral'. From the named person's point of view, some professionals have experienced conflict of loyalty by acting as a named person and as an officer of an LEA and this must be carefully considered in every case (Thomson *et al.*, 1986).

Nicola, aged 2 years 7 months

Nicola has Down's Syndrome. She will begin attending nursery school in five months.

> Presently involved:
> Parents
> Educational psychologist
> Health visitor
> Educational home visitor
> Speech therapist

Choice of named person: The educational home visitor is well placed for this role. She has known the child since birth, is very familiar with local provision and professional agencies and she will remain involved with the family, at least initially, when Nicola goes to nursery school.

Brian, aged 3 years 9 months

Brian has delayed language and suspected moderate learning difficulties. He attends a nursery class where staff must give him extra attention because of behaviour problems. His father left the family home when Brian was a baby and he and his two sisters live with their mother.

    Presently involved:
    Mother
    Educational psychologist
    Speech therapist
    Social worker
    Homemaker
    Health visitor
    Nursery staff

Choice of named person: In this case, the social worker might be selected as named person. She has been intensively involved with the family for several years, since they required a great deal of support even before the father left. She and the health visitor were the first to suspect that Brian might have special needs and alerted the education authority.

Angela, aged 4 years 3 months

Angela is hearing-impaired and is in receipt of a statement under the Education Act 1981. She attends an ordinary nursery class with a small unit attached which caters for four hearing-impaired children.

    Presently involved:
    Parents
    Educational psychologist
    Specialist teacher for hearing-impaired children
    Nursery staff
    Speech therapist

Choice of named person: The teacher for hearing-impaired children would be a suitable named person for Angela. She has daily contact with the child and her parents and a thorough knowledge of her special needs and educational requirements. She will also continue to teach Angela when she moves into reception class in five months' time.

A WIDER ROLE FOR THE SPECIALIST SUPPORT TEAM

United responsibility for children with special needs does not stop at individual assessment, record keeping and monitoring. The contribution to be made by professional agencies to nursery schools and classes will depend on the individual needs and circumstances of each unit but the following general points can be made:

1. Curriculum planning. Educational psychologists and speech therapists are often involved in discussions about nursery curriculum and organisation. Their involvement, together with specialist teachers, is crucial where children with special needs are to attend.
2. Resources. Professional advisers include specialists from education, social work, health services and voluntary agencies, each with their own area of expertise. Nursery staff should be able to obtain practical advice and materials when necessary, either for specific children or for general use. Specialists are also in a position to keep nursery staff informed of new developments and resources and to provide new materials for trial in the nursery if necessary.
3. Evaluation. Educational psychologists are trained in the techniques of objective programme evaluation and can help nursery staff to carry this out.
4. Research. The integration of children with special needs at pre-school level is a relatively new phenomenon and each case is an experiment. Curriculum planning, resources, programme evaluation and the successful outcome of integration are only some of the areas which must receive the attention of researchers. Again, educational psychologists are ideally placed to carry out research and there has been increasing recognition of the need for this within the profession (Savage, 1987; Hellier, 1988). The teaching profession has also become interested in the role of teacher as researcher (Watt, 1983) and this will be discussed in the next chapter.
5. Inservice training. All of the above points can be brought together under the umbrella of inservice training for nursery staff, to which each professional can have some input; this will be discussed more fully in the next chapter.

SUMMARY

This chapter can best be concluded by two excerpts from DES/DHSS Circular 1/83 (DES/DHSS, 1983).

> The assessment of special educational needs is not an end in itself but a means of arriving at a better understanding of a child's learning difficulties for the practical purpose of providing a guide to his education and a basis against which to monitor his progress.
>
> (Section II.4)

> By bringing together the skills, perceptions and insights of professionals in different disciplines, it should be possible to arrive at a more complete understanding of a child's special educational needs. Effective multi-professional work is not easy to achieve. It requires co-operation, collaboration and mutual support. Each professional adviser needs to be aware of the roles of his colleagues and should seek to reach agreement with them on their several roles and functions.
>
> (Section II.34)

—7—

Nursery teachers and nursery nurses: roles and responsibilities

The social climate is ever-changing. The issues that preoccupy political parties, pressure groups and parents will eventually lead to changes in the structure of our national institutions. Government policy and legislation, however, have a tendency to lag one or two decades behind social change, leading to the situation whereby an institution no longer serves the population for which it was established. This is nowhere more clearly illustrated than in the development of pre-school provision in this country.

As discussed in Chapter 1, for historical reasons day care provision and nursery education developed along parallel paths. This artificial distinction between care and education is no longer tenable today, and hence increasing attention is being paid to combined nursery centres and services. The integration of children with special needs into ordinary nurseries cannot be considered in isolation from this trend to provide integrated pre-school provision, and indeed may act as a catalyst for change.

Staffing of pre-school facilities is one of the most contentious areas in this nursery revolution. It is generally accepted that staff are no longer equipped to meet the demands imposed by the children and families in their nurseries. To talk about extending roles and responsibilities may indeed be inadequate, since the time has come for more radical changes. There are still no real solutions to the problem of how pre-school provision should be staffed within this new integrated framework and, in particular, to the problem of the relative roles and status of nursery teachers and nursery nurses.

The issue of staffing will be addressed in this chapter. The skills required by a pre-school practitioner will be summarised and the means of imparting these skills will be examined, with emphasis on inservice training. First, however, it is necessary to examine the current situation in the debate between nursery teaching and nursery nursing.

STAFFING IN INTEGRATED PRE-SCHOOL PROVISION

To reiterate, a nursery class is situated within an infant or primary school and is staffed by a teacher assisted by one or two nursery nurses. A nursery school is a separate entity under the control of a head teacher, with each class in the school staffed by a teacher and one or two nursery nurses. All are employed by the local education authority and work normal school hours and holidays, although nursery teachers receive higher rates of pay than nursery nurses.

Day nurseries are provided by social services departments and are run by matrons or officers-in-charge with the assistance of a deputy and nursery nurses. The Education Act 1980 made it possible for a teacher to be employed in a day nursery on a part-time basis. Day nursery staff work longer hours and have shorter holidays than nursery education staff. Unqualified assistants or auxiliaries may be found in all types of provision, and increasingly so with the introduction of more children with special needs.

The wide discrepancies between teaching and nursery nursing conditions and between conditions for nursery nurses employed by education departments and social services departments have created one of the main barriers to the setting up of integrated services (Ferri *et al.*, 1981). Two closely related professions cannot work side by side under such highly discrepant conditions. In the study carried out by Ferri and her colleagues, each combined nursery centre had experimented with a different staff structure but none had found the ideal solution.

The attempts of one region in Scotland to deal with this dilemma highlight the problems involved. As mentioned in Chapter 1, Strathclyde Region is engaged in setting up an integrated pre-five service (Strathclyde Regional Council, 1985), and has planned to make radical changes in the staffing of this service (Henderson, 1987). All nursery schools, day nurseries and family centres are to be gradually renamed pre-five centres and will offer child care and education as well as family support and parental involvement. All staff are to be on administrative, professional, technical and clerical conditions of service, with a new salary structure based on a single scale allowing access for experience and qualifications. Staff will be renamed officer in charge, deputy officer in charge, pre-five officer and assistant pre-five officer. Pre-five staff will have to undergo inservice training and a new qualifying course will be set up for pre-five services.

Predictably, these proposals have aroused fierce opposition from those who believe that they mark the end of nursery education in the region, led by the Educational Institute of Scotland (the nursery teachers' union). Livingston (1987) presents the case for maintaining teachers in their position of control over any pre-school service and suggests that they will not accept a worsening of their conditions, and that primary teachers would not be attracted to transfer to the nursery sector in future. She argues that the LEA has put forward these plans because of pressure from one dissatisfied group of workers, namely the nursery nurses, but she points out that 'the ideal answer would be to "level up" and improve pay conditions of all the women who work in the pre-five sector, rather than seek to worsen the conditions of another group'. This sentiment is also expressed by Carmichael (1987), who points out that the EIS has 'no objection to other workers being placed on conditions similar to teachers' and 'supports the nursery nurses in their demand for salary regrading'.

Nursery nurses are also lobbying strongly to maintain their autonomy as a separate profession. Collis (1988) discusses the many skills that a nursery nurse can bring to an educational setting. These include stimulation of language development, encouraging social and self-help skills, meeting physical needs, providing emotional security and contributing to curriculum planning. The overlap with a teacher's skills is obvious.

Penn (1987) puts forward the rationale behind Strathclyde Region's proposals and argues that the difficulties are not new and unique to that region, pointing out that 'it is an ambitious project, without precedents in the United Kingdom, and many are hoping to learn from our attempts'. She pinpoints two crucial factors which are required if an integrated pre-five service is to succeed. Firstly, consultation must take place at all levels and it may be necessary to educate practitioners to become better communicators of their ideas and recommendations, since staff are unused to their opinions being sought on broad issues of policy. Secondly, research and development must be integral parts of the programme, involving both academics and practitioners.

Research into the staffing requirements of integrated pre-school provision is certainly urgently required. In addition to the provision of general teaching and care, the integration of children with special needs will require the nursery to provide specialised teaching and care. It will be useful at this point to consider some of the skills that pre-school practitioners will require in order to function in this new service. The word 'practitioner' is used here because no distinction will be made in the following sections between nursery teachers and nursery nurses, unless specifically stated.

SKILLS OF THE PRE-SCHOOL PRACTITIONER

The central feature of the skills which have traditionally been imparted to pre-school practitioners is a thorough knowledge of the stages of normal child development. A nursery practitioner cannot carry out any activities with pre-school children without a detailed understanding of cognitive ability, language processes, social skills and emotional development as they relate to children within the age range of pre-school education. This knowledge allows the practitioner to plan a general curriculum, identify children with special needs and communicate with other professionals in the pre-school field. Training courses have generally covered these areas in some detail and will continue to do so.

The following topics and issues represent those areas where change and expansion are most urgently needed.

1. Special needs. It is obvious that nursery staff will require to be knowledgeable about the problems facing children with special needs and the ways in which these needs can be met.

2. Assessment and record keeping. As fully discussed in Chapter 6, assessment and record keeping should be essential activities in all pre-school units, particularly for children with special needs.

3. Self-evaluation. Students are always observed in the nursery by their tutors with a view to improving their practice. This process should not stop. Staff can always learn and develop new and better ways of interacting with children by self-observation and by observing each other (Katz, 1985).

4. Research. The need for research has been brought up repeatedly throughout this book and the nursery practitioner is ideally placed to take part in and even carry out research. Unfortunately, it is the case that 'few teachers have been trained to assess the effectiveness of the practices they introduce' (Tizard *et al.*, 1981).

5. Working with other professionals. Nursery staff must be able to interact with a large number of other professionals, as outlined in Chapter 6. For such contacts to be effective, the nursery practitioner must have some knowledge of the areas of expertise offered by each professional agency. Links will have to be established with teachers in special education so that ideas can be exchanged. Nursery teachers and nursery nurses must also have a clearer understanding of each other's training and skills.

6. Parents. Nursery staff must be able to work with parents in a variety of ways. They must know how to support and advise families and they must also be open to ways of involving parents in their children's education and learning from parents who are perhaps skilled in dealing with their own child's special needs.

7. Leadership skills. Under the present system of pre-school provision, nursery teachers in particular require leadership skills, since they will always be working in situations where they are responsible for organising other professionals, paraprofessionals and parents.

8. Visitors. Nursery practitioners are very well aware of the pressures created by the constant stream of visitors who invade their nurseries. This invasion must be controlled if the children are not to be seriously disrupted by the numbers of strange adults present at any one time. Visitors range from young secondary school and college students seeking work experience to trainees from a range of professions, such as social workers, doctors, health visitors, speech therapists and teachers from a variety of backgrounds. It is important that nursery staff do try to accommodate and educate interested visitors, since this helps to foster good relationships between the professions and greater understanding of the role of pre-school education.

9. Isolation. It is unfortunate but true that many pre-school practitioners feel isolated from the mainstream of education and child care. The nursery class teacher in a primary school might have few opportunities for interaction with colleagues in the 'main school' because the nursery is often a separate, self contained unit (Heaslip, 1987). Infant and primary teachers are also often ignorant of the aims and objectives of nursery education and do not consider nursery teachers to be real 'educators'. A nursery nurse in a nursery class is likely to be even more isolated, since there might be no other nursery nurses in the school and no provision made for contact with colleagues in other schools or nurseries. Nursery practitioners must be aware of this isolation and prepared to deal with it.

POSITIVE ATTITUDES

In a questionnaire completed by 84 Oregon administrators responsible for special education, they were asked to list problems involved in setting up integration programmes (Warnock, 1976). Top of the list were problems of negative attitudes towards the programme and integration generally, mentioned by 81 per cent of respondents.

Positive staff attitude is the most crucial factor in determining the outcome of any project aimed at integrating children with special needs. Every necessary resource can be provided but if the staff, and particularly the person-in-charge, are not fully supportive, the project is destined to failure. Even if staff have positive attitudes towards the concept of integration, they may not have appropriate attitudes and beliefs about the needs of the children to be integrated and their role in meeting these needs. Clark (1976) was interested in staff attitudes before, during and after a project that involved the integration of mentally and physically handicapped children into an ordinary nursery class. It was found that teacher attitudes expressed before the project were often inappropriate and were modified throughout the integration experience. Examples of preconceived ideas that had to be altered included:

1. Class routines need not be modified to accommodate integration.
2. All children within a particular category will respond in concert to a particular educational methodology.
3. Sufficient insight by staff will enable any child to respond within the parameters of normality.
4. Physically handicapped children are easier to accommodate than mentally handicapped.

Gipps (1982b) states that 'there has been little systematic work in this country on the attitude of staff towards pre-school children and their families' and she reports findings from a survey of nursery nurses' and nursery teachers' attitudes towards children and their parents, many from socially disadvantaged backgrounds. It was concluded that 'day nursery nurses expressed more sympathetic attitudes towards both children and parents than did their colleagues in centres and schools, while teachers had more sympathetic attitudes than nursery nurses'. Gipps suggested that 'these attitudes must, in however subtle a manner, affect their working relationship with the parents and therefore their children'. Ways of overcoming this barrier to a good working relationship will be discussed in the next chapter.

INITIAL TRAINING

The above list of skills and requirements for pre-school practitioners, which is by no means exhaustive, should allay any misconceptions that pre-school education in the 1980s is no more than 'babyminding' and watching children play. Nursery teachers require all the skills of their colleagues in other sectors of education, as well as skills that are unique to their particular situation, and their training should reflect this. Nursery nurses in day nurseries now deal almost exclusively with children who have special needs because of difficult home circumstances.

Nursery teachers

Teachers come into nursery education through a great diversity of channels, some being more prepared for the job than others.

As Livingston (1987) points out, 'Scotland is one of the few countries in the world which has always required its nursery teachers to attain the same standard of academic and professional training as primary teachers and to undertake a post-initial specialist training as well'.

The situation in England is less uniform. Clark *et al.* (1982) interviewed the head teachers of 10 nursery schools and the teachers in charge of 41 nursery classes in Birmingham and Coventry. Four of the nursery school head teachers and almost half of the nursery class teachers had received infant/junior training with no pre-school component. One nursery class teacher had only taught mathematics at secondary level before being appointed to her present post.

Nursery nurses

Most nursery nurses in this country hold a certificate of the National Nursery Examination Board (NNEB) or its Scottish equivalent (SNNEB). Courses are generally held in colleges of further education and are open to all who have reached school-leaving age.

Some concern has been expressed in recent years about the number of Youth Training Schemes that are being set up and which offer diplomas in nursery nursing after two years of 'training' (Hevey, reported by Hagedorn, 1986). These courses are uncoordinated, with no regulation of the content, and have created what Hevey describes as the 'great training muddle'. Hevey's most radical suggestion to remedy this situation is the setting up of one single unified body responsible for setting standards and overseeing all under-five training. Different levels of competence would be incorporated within this single system. Both Hevey and Heaslip (1987) stress the potential of the National Council for Vocational Qualifications for raising standards and improving the level of training received by nursery nurses.

Satisfaction with initial training

Not surprisingly, many practitioners in the studies mentioned above felt that their initial training had not prepared them for the posts that they held. Clark *et al.* (1982) found that half of the nursery teachers interviewed expressed dissatisfaction with their training and most frequently mentioned that they would have appreciated more training in administration, the handling of staff and planning the curriculum. Similarly, 81 per cent of day nursery matrons and officers-in-charge were dissatisfied with their initial training, most feeling that it no longer related to the type of children with whom they were then working.

An extensive survey was carried out more recently in Avon, in which nursery head teachers, nursery teachers and nursery nurses were asked to comment on their training (Heaslip, 1985). It was found that, 'almost without exception, teachers interviewed commented on the lack of relevance of their initial training to their role in the nursery' (Heaslip, 1987). Heaslip presents some typical comments from teacher interviews, two of which are included here:

> My teacher training was nursery/infant but it really was all infant – there was hardly any nursery in it at all except teaching practice – otherwise it was quite good training. There was nothing at all on working with nursery nurses and very little on what to do with parents.

> My training was abysmal. I learnt nothing on relationships, nothing about working with nursery nurses. Nursery nurses came as a terrific shock to me ... I didn't know whether they were medical assistants or what. Parents weren't even mentioned.

Heaslip pointed out that criticism of training did not relate to any particular decade since staff who were recently trained made similar comments to those trained several decades ago.

It has already been mentioned that nursery nurses do not feel adequately trained to deal with the many children with special needs who now attend their nurseries and this also applies to nursery teachers. Clark *et al.* (1982) found that 'the majority of those interviewed had no training or experience related to children with special needs'. They went on to say that:

> There was also very little specialist knowledge amongst the ordinary staff in the units. It is not, therefore, surprising that most of those interviewed felt that their training had not prepared them for dealing with handicapped children in their units. Most said they had never been to a nursery for children with special needs. For those who did report contact with handicapped children, either in training or since, it tended to be in the form of a one-off visit to observe.

The fact that nursery teachers are so critical of their initial training might be related to the growing concern about the quality of the staff who train them. B. Tizard (1975) quoted Bernstein (1975), who believed that the training of nursery teachers did not help them to understand the principles of basic education and learning, and the situation is worse today. The British Association for Early Childhood Education has been concerned for several years about the growing shortage of early years trainers. Vacancies for early years tutors are either not being filled or are being filled with unsuitable candidates. Heaslip (1987) attributes this to the fact that:

> there is still in many training institutions a patronising approach to early childhood education and little more than nominal recognition of the importance of having courses led by appropriate staff … Subject specialists and those with secondary orientation almost automatically by tradition take priority over staff with early years specialism when new appointments are being made.

There is very little real research evidence to suggest that the gloomy picture just painted is not representative of the scene elsewhere in England, in spite of the Nursery Education Research Programme Committee's suggestion, almost 13 years ago, 'that the time is ripe to institute a project to develop and monitor courses of initial training for teachers of young children, with particular reference to the needs of nursery teachers' (DES, 1975). This research project is even more urgently required in the light of the Warnock Report and the Education Act 1981.

Requirements of initial teacher training

The discussion of initial training has highlighted many of its shortcomings and has identified areas of priority, which can be summarised as follows:

1. Teachers must be trained for pre-school education. This statement seems so obvious that it should not have to be made. Primary teachers have always been trained to teach in primary schools and secondary teachers for secondary schools, yet the requirement that pre-school teachers should be trained to teach in nurseries has not been nationally accepted.
2. Trainers of pre-school teachers must have experience and expertise in pre-school education.
3. The first two requirements will only be met if colleges recognise the importance of early years training and allocate necessary resources.
4. The content of initial training courses must be relevant to the demands facing nursery staff in the 1980s, giving the skills that have been discussed throughout this chapter.
5. Students must be encouraged to view initial training as only the first phase of professional and personal development, this

being a process which should continue throughout a teacher's career (Taylor, 1980). The greatest contribution to continuing professional growth will be provided through inservice training.

INSERVICE TRAINING

Changes in the content and quality of initial training will eventually be reflected in changes in nursery practice but this process will be slow. Existing staff are having to cope with new demands now and effective inservice training has never been more urgently required. The integration of children with special needs is forging ahead and the skills of staff are not keeping pace. This is clearly illustrated by McQuaid (1986), who reported that Ulster would shortly be admitting severely handicapped children to mainstream schools and that this would require that 'both teachers' and other pupils' attitudes towards handicap will have to be overhauled'. This article appeared in November 1986 and concluded that 'the boards (of education) had a duty to learn by April (1987) how to provide for a "client population" which had not previously been their responsibility'. Inservice education is not, therefore, preparing staff for a future situation. Their client population has already changed, often with little preparation.

Just as research into initial training has received low priority, so there are few major studies looking at the area of pre-school staff development. The Education of the Developmentally Young project at the Hester Adrian Research Centre produced a handbook and workbooks to train nursery staff in behavioural methods (McBrien and Foxen, 1981). Part of the Oxford Pre-School Research Project led to a training booklet to teach staff the basic components of direct observational techniques (Sylva *et al.*, 1979). Inservice training in language and communication skills may be assisted by material produced by Robson (1979) and McConkey (1980).

Conventional inservice education

The most significant trend in the provision of inservice education has been to move away from conventional courses and conferences to school-based training where all staff members can become involved.

Inservice training has traditionally been the focus of a great deal of criticism. It was something provided for promoted staff but not readily available to the majority of teachers. The content was often felt to be irrelevant to the needs of the staff. A package would be offered to teachers. Having digested the package, the teachers would have a set of skills to apply to any situation. The result of this kind of approach is inflexible teaching and an inability to respond appropriately when specific needs arise (Nixon, 1981).

Cameron (1988) argues strongly for radical changes in the whole concept of inservice training and staff development, stating that we are still entrenched in the notion that teachers, once trained, are autonomous 'professionals' who have nothing more to learn. She goes on to say that, within this framework, inservice training is 'intended to help aspiring teachers to gain promotion, or to help promoted teachers justify their position by having more of the "mystery" to pass on'. If the current economic climate means that promotion is much more difficult to achieve, there is still the 'lingering cynicism that teachers are not interested in professional development but merely in skiving'. Comments such as these will be familiar to most teachers but Cameron (1988) and Watt (1983) argue that it is time to re-examine attitudes towards inservice training. Ever-diminishing promotion prospects can make teachers determined to gain as many qualifications as possible. More importantly, however, teachers have seen the need for inservice training to give them new skills to meet new demands. Inservice training will only be acceptable if it is relevant to their own situation.

Inservice training for nursery nurses

If teachers have generally felt disillusioned about inservice training, the situation for nursery nurses is even gloomier. Halloran (1982) found that 61 per cent of nursery nurses under the age of 30 in his research sample had not undertaken any form of inservice training. Moreover, many were working in the same nursery in which they had been students. Heaslip (1987) reports similar findings from his survey, attributing non-attendance at inservice courses to the lack of career structure for nursery nurses, who saw inservice training as 'an avenue for enhancing career prospects'. The opportunities for staff development are, therefore, virtually non-existent and this is doubly worrying in view of reported dissatisfaction by nursery nurses of their initial training.

Millward (1988) suggests that the nursery nursing profession should take responsibility for its own inservice training, but the counter-argument by Collis (1988) is more convincing. The latter states that 'if a whole school approach is to be achieved it is vital that teachers and nursery nurses attend courses together'.

A FRAMEWORK FOR INSERVICE EDUCATION

It is impossible to discuss all forms of inservice education. Formal qualifications and requirements differ in England and Scotland. Local authorities have developed their own initiatives and programmes. Much innovative work is carried out within single nursery centres and the results are transmitted to others in the locality. The following categories of training give some examples of the types of inservice training that can be offered. Training should be available for teachers *and* nursery nurses unless specifically stated, as in the case of formal qualifications, where the two professions follow different courses at the present time.

Further qualifications

Further qualifications open to nursery teachers should fall into two broad areas, the first compulsory and the second voluntary.

Diploma or Certificate in Pre-School Education

It is strongly advocated that nursery teachers should hold a formal qualification in pre-school education, having completed a full-time (one year) or part-time (two years) course of study.

In June 1987 the Roehampton Institute of Education opened a Centre for Early Childhood Studies and teachers can apply to study for an Advanced Diploma. Dixon (1987) discusses some other initiatives in the field of early education. A new diploma in multidisciplinary approaches to young children and their families is being developed in the East Midlands. A Certificate of Professional Development in Pre-School Work is being offered at Liverpool Polytechnic.

Diploma or Certificate in Special Needs

These are courses which lead to a diploma, advanced diploma or master's degree and are generally undertaken as one year full-time or two year part-time modes. Specific examples of these courses are given by Wolfendale (1987). They are generally aimed at primary education but many allow special studies to be undertaken in pre-schools. A few courses have been set up specifically for nursery staff. An example is the Special Qualification Course in Nursery Education at Moray House College of Education in Edinburgh. The course is offered as a block release for teachers who have at least three years' experience.

The Open University offer a course entitled 'Special Needs in Education', which has been widely followed (see Booth, 1985; Hegarty, 1987).

NNEB Certificate of Post Qualifying Studies

This college-based course has been introduced during the past five years in an attempt to raise the standard of nursery nursing and keep nursery nurses up to date in the skills they offer. It remains to be seen whether employers will also make use of this advanced qualification to improve the career structure within nursery nursing.

Specialist courses and conferences

Voluntary organisations run national, regional and local conferences which are open to all disciplines. These include the Down's Children's Association, MENCAP and the Spastics Society (Wolfendale, 1987).

Professional associations also run courses and conferences that aim to bring together several disciplines to share ideas and learn from each other. An example would be a one day conference in 1987 that was run by a branch of the British Psychological Society to discuss special needs in pre-school education, and that was attended by psychologists, teachers, speech therapists, physiotherapists, health service staff and, most importantly, parents.

Courses may be run locally to introduce nursery staff to new packages that have been developed. Workshops may be set up to allow staff to practise new skills and techniques and evaluate their own and each other's performance. Of relevance to pre-school education might be EDY and Portage, which have been discussed in this and previous chapters.

Local education authorities

All LEAs must provide some inservice training for their pre-school staff in the light of the Education Act 1981. Advisers and educational psychologists develop short courses which should reflect the needs of staff in their particular nurseries. An increasing number of LEAs are producing packages which incorporate a comprehensive inservice programme, including booklets, video tapes and materials for use in schools. With names like SNAP (Coventry Special Needs Action Programme) and SNIP (Essex Special Needs Information Package), these programmes are aimed at the full range of primary education but contain information relevant to pre-school education.

It is important that other LEAs do not blindly adopt packages developed elsewhere without looking closely at the content and its relevance to their areas. How far the packages are successful in achieving their aims should be closely evaluated by the team responsible for introducing them (Clarke, 1987).

Practitioner participation

It has repeatedly been stated that teachers and nursery nurses know what their needs are in terms of inservice training. They will only be receptive to conventional courses and conferences if they feel that these are going to be directly useful to them on the job. Practitioner participation in inservice training can be enhanced in four important ways:

1. Joint planning. Nursery teachers and nursery nurses should be consulted and actively involved in planning and evaluating LEA-initiated inservice programmes.
2. School-based development work. Where possible, workshops and courses should be carried out in nurseries.
3. Teacher as researcher. Teachers have long complained that researchers ask the wrong questions, reach the wrong conclusions and fail to make any real impact on education in the classroom. Researchers have been frustrated by the apparent refusal of the teaching profession to adopt new methods in response to research findings. The 'teacher as researcher' movement is an attempt to overcome this communication problem between research and practice. It is the ultimate form of school-based, teacher-directed, inservice education. 'It assumes that the teacher will be active, questioning, critical and initiating' (Watt, 1983). Some literature is now available to help teachers plan and carry out action research (e.g. Nixon, 1981; Hopkins, 1984a, b, 1985).
4. Collaborative participation within the education system. Watt (1983) stresses the need to reduce the sense of isolation from the rest of the teaching profession that nursery teachers feel. Nursery teachers must spend time in discussion with infant and primary school teachers. The exchange of ideas and learning about each other's perspectives can be rewarding in terms of personal satisfaction gained from being part of a professional community with common aims. Continuity of educational experience for children will also be more meaningful.

Pre-school education has so far played little part in the participatory model of inservice education, but where it has occurred the results seem to be favourable. Research projects directed by Tough (1977) and Manning and Sharp (1977) involved the active co-operation of many nursery teachers throughout the country and the response was very enthusiastic. On a more limited scale, the Oxford Pre-School Research Project (Bruner, 1980) gave nursery staff the opportunity to participate in, and to some extent control the direction of, research projects, again with some success. Nursery staff generally have no training in research methods and so considerable support must be given by researchers or educational psychologists, at least in the initial stages of a project. It is, therefore, too early to say whether participatory inservice training of this nature will be a viable option. There would certainly seem to be a demand for research methods to be included in teacher training, perhaps even at the initial stages.

Learning day by day

Finally, inservice education should not be seen only in terms of diplomas, packages, conferences, courses or even participatory learning. Nursery staff should be open on a daily basis to absorb new information and to learn from those around them. Every case conference they attend will provide new insights. Watching a psychologist or speech therapist carry out an assessment or simply interact with a child will provide a different perspective. Discussions with other teachers from a wide range of backgrounds will provide new information. Some parents will be able to demonstrate their expertise with their own child.

PRE-SCHOOL STAFF TRAINING: A LONG-TERM PERSPECTIVE

The expertise and training of pre-school practitioners have been discussed in some detail but the problem outlined at the beginning of this chapter has not been resolved, namely the reconciliation of two professions working closely together but with a separate identity. The historical differences between teachers and nursery nurses will make it a difficult problem to resolve. In practice, however, the differences between teachers and nursery nurses are not nearly so apparent, to the extent that an outsider entering a nursery school is unlikely to be able to identify which adults are teachers and which are nursery nurses. Each profession puts forward a case for the unique contribution that it can make to pre-school education and care but there is considerable overlap in areas of expertise, as already discussed.

The growth of combined nursery centres will continue to put pressure on employers, administrators and unions to reach an agreement about staffing. Understandably, teachers will not wish to see a decline in their working conditions to match those of nursery nurses. Teachers' unions have expressed their support for nursery nurses in their battle for improved pay and conditions but they are unlikely to accept equal status with a profession that is seen to be less well qualified. Some nursery nurses do move into teaching but, with only 2 per cent of nursery nurse candidates possessing one or more 'A' level (Brierley, 1981), there will be 'little prospect of enhanced status or career prospects in the education sector for the majority of NNEB certificate holders' (Heaslip, 1987). The National Council for Vocational Qualifications is urged to consider the raising of the standard of applicants for nursery nursing courses.

Just as the distinction between pre-school education and care is no longer tenable, so the distinction between educators and carers in combined nursery centres is equally inappropriate. Strathclyde Region is heading in the right direction by advocating a single training course to prepare for a unified pre-school profession. The strength of opposition mounted against this proposal suggests that pre-school education is not yet ready for such sweeping, radical changes.

8

Roles for parents

Parental involvement is more often preached than practised.
McConkey (1983)

It is certainly the case that parental involvement in children's education has been preached at great length during the past two decades. A short browse through the literature on parents and education would give the impression that parents are now actively involved at all levels of the system, from pre-school to secondary schools, from policy making to assessment and classroom teaching. Gone are the days when the annual parents' night was the sum total of a parent's involvement in school. Parents now enjoy more powerful legal rights in relation to their child's education than at any time in the past and indeed, 'parent power' is the popular phrase presently expounded by politicians who are reacting to an ever-growing popular movement in this direction.

It would seem reasonable to suggest that parental involvement should be easier to accomplish in pre-school education than in the later years. Nurseries are less formal, do not work to strict timetables and should be more flexible in accommodating parents. It is very difficult to obtain a national picture of the extent of parental involvement in pre-school education since there are no official statistics. It is certainly true that when researchers have set up research projects specifically to involve parents, the response is generally reported to be very enthusiastic. On the other hand, McConkey and others have suggested that parental participation is not as widely accepted and practised as suggested by the rhetoric.

This chapter will look in some detail at parental involvement in pre-school education. The nature of the 'partnership' between parents and professionals will be considered in terms of the roles of each and the capacity for mutual support and benefits. Major initiatives in parental involvement will be discussed, highlighting some of the requirements for successful partnership. It will then be possible to draw together these various strands of evidence to suggest how a nursery might begin to improve its working relationship with parents, the emphasis being on detailed planning and individual assessment of family needs. First, however, let us define 'parent'.

WHO ARE THE PARENTS?

The literature on parental involvement in education frequently discusses parents as if they were a uniform mass of people with common aims and a common identity. We are, therefore, told what parents wish, what parents need and what parents should be doing. The individuality of parents and families is not stressed and nor is the complex issue of the changing needs of parents in relation to their acceptance and understanding of their child's special needs. Obviously researchers and writers are aware that these individual differences exist but they need to make them much more explicit, or parents and nursery staff alike will feel that they have failed if their 'partnership' is not thriving and doing all the things that they have been told should be done.

First of all, consider parental expectations when they enrol their child in the nursery:

1. Parents may have received intensive help and guidance from a home visiting teacher for many months.
2. They may have refused all offers of assistance, attendance at nursery being their first contact with the education department.
3. They may not have accepted that their child has special needs.
4. They may not have wanted their child to attend nursery, but brought the child because of pressure from their health visitor, social worker or family.

These are only a few examples of parental experience and expectations, each of which will result in a very different relationship with nursery staff.

Family background and other commitments and stresses also influence the nature of the staff/parent partnership. Imagine a 3-year-old Down's Syndrome child attending an ordinary nursery school. It might be argued that, in an ideal world, this child would live in the locality of the nursery with both parents. One parent would be working and the other would be at home all day. There would be no other pre-school children in the family. One parent would be able to spend time in the nursery and develop a good working relationship with staff. The other would be interested and involved when possible. In the real world, however, the child could come from any of the following homes:

1. Mother is 19 years old, unmarried and unsupported.
2. Mother has four other children to care for, including two others under 5 years. Father is unemployed, drinks heavily

and frequently leaves the family home.

3. Father is a business executive who travels widely. Mother is a solicitor and an active partner in a firm of solicitors. Two older children attend boarding school. The child is cared for by a childminder until mother returns from work.

4. Father works long hours and has not been seen by nursery staff. Mother does not speak English and is reluctant to linger in the nursery.

5. Mother is unmarried and attended a special school herself. She does not read and cannot handle her child, whose behaviour is very disruptive. She is keen to stay in the nursery all day and takes up considerable staff time.

6. Mother is a nursery nurse who worked in a special school but is presently not working. She has two older children and is keen to become involved in the nursery but lives six miles away and has no transport.

Clearly, the potential for parental involvement is very different in each of the above families. Chazan *et al.* (1980) discuss some of the problems facing families in their research sample. Factors relating to their child with special needs included toilet problems, sleep problems, overactivity, destructiveness, demanding behaviour and aggression. Other stresses in the families 'ranged from difficulties faced by one-parent families, mother's ill health and problems with siblings to poor housing, marital problems and the mismanagement of resources'. Smith (1980) expresses concern about the lack of effort to find ways of involving working mothers. In her study of parents and pre-school, which formed part of the Oxford Pre-School Research Project, she found that some nursery staff made negative comments about mothers going back to work too soon or using the nursery to 'dump' their children. On the other hand, she states that 'working parents often regretted the difficulties of being involved or felt guilty about not putting in their fair share of effort'.

Staff should also be alert to the reasons for a parent showing unwillingness to become involved in the nursery. The parent may indeed have no desire to become involved, but Ferri *et al.* (1981) found that many of the 25 per cent of the mothers in their sample who were unenthusiastic about involvement were, in fact, embarrassed and lacking in confidence and could not approach staff.

The remainder of this chapter will consider many of the ways in which parents can become involved in the nursery. All parents will have some form of relationship with staff. None are expected to be involved in all the ways that will be discussed. The nature of the partnership will fluctuate according to the needs of the child, family and staff at any given time.

AN EQUAL PARTNERSHIP?

A successful partnership is based on equality, whereby each partner recognises and benefits from the talents, skills, expertise and knowledge of the other. At times one partner may adopt a relatively passive role, in other situations a more active role.

The relationship between teacher and parent has traditionally been unequal, even within pre-school education. Neither party would have called the relationship a partnership, since the teacher clearly enjoyed a much higher status than the parent in matters relating to a child's education. The teacher was the expert and the parent could only listen and observe in awe, as illustrated by guidelines on parent/teacher relations issued by the Department of Education and Science in 1968. Nursery teachers give advice to parents on social matters and help them to sort out their many domestic problems. Meetings are arranged so that staff can explain to parents their 'dos and don'ts' and tell them about the forthcoming 'harvest sale' and Christmas party. The highlight of the school year is the summer term, when mothers come in and see what is done. While most of the parents' involvement is passive, it is noted that 'many nursery schools have found them [the parents] willing to help, for example, with the mending and making of toys and apparatus'.

This all sounds very old-fashioned and our thinking would appear to have developed considerably during the two decades since this document appeared. But has nursery practice really changed all that much? The Warnock Report includes a chapter entitled 'Parents as Partners' and advocates that parents should be given information, advice and support, practical help and relief from the stress of the daily care of their child. Certainly, all these factors are essential considerations and will be discussed later, but the partnership is surely one-sided and unequal if we do not consider what parents can give.

Mortimer (1986) gives advice to nursery teachers who are accepting a child with special needs. Quite correctly, they are urged to talk to the parents before admission, since 'they are the experts on their own child'. They are advised that 'parents can be usefully used to show you how they cope with the child's needs for the first week or so until you feel confident to take over' and they should continue to use parents for longer if they need more information. The teacher should then go on to make a plan for the child, including assessment, record keeping and a programme of activities to be carried out and monitored. Parents are no longer mentioned and by the end of the article the term *your* special child is used. The parents' expertise is obviously no longer necessary, the teacher has taken over.

In their West Midlands study, Clark *et al.* (1982) asked staff in nursery schools and classes about the extent of parental involvement. In 70 per cent of the nursery schools and 54 per cent of the nursery classes parents were used at some time for general assistance and tidying up but not for specific tasks with the children. The remainder did not involve parents in any meaningful way. Teachers in nine units, mainly nursery classes, specifically stated that they did not want parents to come into the nursery because 'parents required too much staff time in organising them and telling them what to do and, moreover, they tended to be a disruptive influence on their own children'.

Other studies have found that staff have not always been positive in their attitudes towards parents (Ferri *et al.*, 1981; Gipps, 1982b). Watt (1983) would attribute this to a failure of initial training courses to give teachers the skills necessary for working with parents and she sees this as the most important area for inservice education. She claims that there is little real enthusiasm within the teaching profession for parental involvement and quotes Tizard *et al.* (1981), who maintained that 'college tutors, heads and advisers are likely to give more weight to the quality of the young teacher's wall displays than to her attempts to foster relationships with parents'.

STAFF SUPPORT FOR PARENTS

Counselling

Parents may use nursery staff as counsellors. This requires that staff have some empathy with parents, a genuine willingness to understand their needs and the ability to listen. If necessary, staff should be able to direct parents to other agencies according to their needs (Threfall, 1979).

Resources

Nursery staff need some knowledge about the resources available for parents. Parents may ask about the provision of practical help, financial assistance or the availability of respite care for their child.

Information

Staff should provide a full account of the aims and curriculum of the nursery. They also need to be knowledgeable about other forms of pre-school provision, special education and the infant classroom, since parents will have questions about alternative and future education.

Encouragement to participate

Staff must continually look for ways to encourage parents to take the first step towards involvement. This might involve formal open days and parents' meetings. More often it will mean being accessible to parents so that they have opportunities to build up a relationship. If a parent is known to have a particular skill, staff might capitalise on that.

Group leadership

Parent groups can be extremely supportive but they may need to be initiated by staff. The group leader must be enthusiastic, confident and resourceful and if the nursery staff feel that they do not have the necessary skills, they might call on a social worker or psychologist to initiate group work. They can then learn through observation.

Teaching new skills

Staff may be able to provide parents with new ideas for working with their child in the nursery or at home. This may take the form of a structured programme with specific goals, or it may be more informal, passing on tips and suggestions.

PARENTAL SUPPORT FOR STAFF

Parent as demonstrator

Parents can show staff how they handle their child at home. They might pass on information that they have received from home teachers, speech therapists, psychologists or physiotherapists, although nursery staff should also receive this information directly from these agencies.

Parent as teacher and assessor

Parents may become involved in their child's learning programme, helping the child in the nursery and at home and assisting staff to monitor progress.

Parent as group leader

Parents may be able to organise or participate in parent groups based in the nursery. The group's aim might be purely social, such as planning outings and fundraising events. Alternatively, the principal aim might be to hold discussions and mutually supportive counselling sessions.

Parent as staff trainer

This is possibly the most ambitious role for parents and is not a common feature of staff/parent relationships in the nursery, but it has considerable potential. Staff feel ill-equipped to deal with the needs and demands of parents of children with special needs so why don't parents themselves help to train the staff? Willing and able parents could attend inservice meetings and courses to talk to staff and answer their questions. Mittler (1983) goes one step further by suggesting that:

> parent groups at local and national level might make a formal approach to institutes of higher education such as universities, polytechnics and colleges, as well as to professional associations involved in training, in order to enquire about the extent to which the training of professionals includes some degree of awareness and preparation for working with parents.

PRE-SCHOOL INITIATIVES IN PARENTAL INVOLVEMENT

Parent workshops

Pioneering work in this area was carried out in Manchester at the Hester Adrian Research Centre in the early 1970s. The first workshops were for parents of pre-school children with learning difficulties and ran for 14 sessions of 2½ hours' duration. The aims of the workshops were to give parents new skills in observing their children, assessing specific needs, selecting tasks and evaluating progress. Teaching was by means of small tutorial groups and lectures and a final meeting six months after the course had ended allowed the team to assess the effectiveness of the programme. Attendance was high and parents seemed to benefit from their involvement. Subsequent projects throughout the country have been modelled on the Hester Adrian work-shops, although the majority have focused on school-aged children. Attwood (1977, 1978) ran workshops in Croydon for the parents of pre-school children with learning difficulties. Pugh (1981a) summarises some of the lessons to be learnt from these projects:

1. Workshops should be based in schools and involve staff to help build up a trusting relationship between parents and staff.
2. Careful planning and structuring are essential but there must also be some flexibility to allow individual parent's needs to be met as they arise.
3. The whole experience for parents must be positive and confidence boosting. This means that contributers must be well organised. If a large multi-disciplinary team is involved they must meet between each session to discuss the previous session and plan ahead. Tutors must be able to handle discussions sensitively without dominating the group and should allow parents to take over as much as possible.
4. Tutors should meet the parents before the course starts to discover the areas of greatest need.
5. Tutors should also visit the child before the course starts and continue to monitor the child's progress throughout.
6. Parents benefit from having access to a multi-disciplinary team, meeting those professionals who will possibly be involved with their child at some time. Most workshops have been organised by psychologists with assistance from teachers, health visitors, social workers, speech therapists and others with expertise relevant to the topics being discussed.
7. The most popular format for the workshop seems to be group discussion, with a lecture given by a single speaker the least popular.
8. The professionals involved must have a long-term commitment to working with the parents in the group. It is not enough to give parents a few weeks of intensive support and encouragement and then to withdraw.

Parent involvement project

This project began in 1973 at the Hester Adrian Research Centre, following on from the parent workshops. Again the aim was to help parents to assess the developmental level of their own children and to select activities which would help them progress to the next stages (McConkey *et al.*, 1979). Tapes were used so that parents could analyse their own interactions with their children and learn new skills. The many teaching games devised during this study were incorporated in the popular resource books *Let Me Speak* (Jeffree and McConkey, 1976) and *Let Me Play* (Jeffree *et al.*, 1977).

The Anson House pre-school project

This project was set up at the Hester Adrian Research Centre in 1975. The nursery provision at Anson House has brought together a wide range of children, from those who are profoundly and multiply handicapped to those with no apparent developmental delay (Gunstone *et al.*, 1982). An important focus of the project has been parental involvement, aimed at increasing parents' confidence in their own expertise and knowledge of their children and ensuring that they are fully informed about the role of different professionals and the means of contacting these agencies. Parents attend the nursery regularly and work alongside staff with their children. They meet each other and a wide range of professionals who are readily available to them.

Beveridge (1983) outlines the service model, which begins by looking at the needs of the parents and staff. The model for parental involvement incorporates five major areas:

Social work support.
Exchange of information.
Parent participation within the team.
Developing parent–child relationships.
Liaison between families and community networks and resources.

Beveridge (1983) summarises these five components of the service; full details are contained in Beveridge *et al.* (1982). Sebba (1980) examines the effectiveness of training parents to follow a programme with their child at home.

Two important areas for concern arise from the project. Firstly, there is a need to focus on the whole family and its relationship to the community, not just on the child with special needs. Secondly, every family is different. Parents have their own individual ways of interacting with their children, some being directive, others being facilitative. These differences must be taken into account by those helping parents to work with their children and parents should not be forced into roles and ways of handling their children which seem totally unnatural to them.

Finally, an interesting feature of parental involvement at Anson House was the accessibility that parents had to files and records kept on their own children, to the extent that they saw reports first and had the opportunity to correct them if necessary. Permission is sought to share the contents of any confidential reports received from professionals. Such openness and honesty must surely reinforce the bonds between parents and staff and enhance their partnership.

Video courses

One of the team from the Hester Adrian Research Centre went to Dublin and continued work with pre-school mentally handicapped children and their families. McConkey developed two 'video courses' entitled *Putting Two Words Together* and *Let's Play*. The former aims to help parents to develop their child's language and the latter emphasises the link between play and learning (McConkey, 1983).

Groups of parents take the course as a series of evening meetings held weekly under the direction of tutors, usually psychologists or therapists. The videos show parents new ways of interacting with children who have special needs, presenters explain what is happening and parents take part in a practical activity. McConkey (1983) stresses that 'explanation must accompany observation', whether parents are watching a video or observing a teacher at work. Practical activities to be carried out at home are an essential feature of the course. The course comes as a complete package which can be used by tutors who require a minimum of training. It is suggested that the material would be useful as part of an inservice training programme for nursery staff. A common course for parents and staff would seem to be most effective, ensuring that the same approach is used in school and at home. McConkey proposes that those with experience of parental involvement should devote 'some of their time to "packaging" their knowledge. Video may be the most effective medium.'

Renfrew and Delta programmes

These programmes were set up to encourage parents to stimulate their children's language development at home. The first courses were organised in Renfrewshire in Scotland during the 1970s (Donachy, 1976, 1979). The main components of the projects were:

1. Parents met regularly with teachers.
2. Parents selected a book from a specially organised library to read with their child at home.
3. Parents were provided each week with a typed unit of a programme to administer at home, outlining materials and

activities to develop general vocabulary, number concepts and understanding of time, space and size.

4. Parents were requested to spend 30 minutes daily on the book activity and programme.
5. At weekly group meetings parents were asked how their last session had gone and exchanged ideas and suggestions.

It is interesting that although the specific aims of the project related to teaching new skills to parents so that they might teach their children, 'discussions at group meetings often ranged over wider aspects of education and child rearing and mothers appeared to be sufficiently reinforced by these meetings to persist in the programme' (Donachy, 1979). This again highlights the need for project organisers to be flexible, in order to allow parents to fulfil their own needs as well as comply with the requirements of the programme.

This intervention was found to increase children's cognitive and language functioning as measured by performance on standard tests. The programme has been further developed in Northern Ireland, where it is entitled the Delta programme (Donachy, 1987). As well as the pre-school programme (3½–5 years), there is now also a toddler programme (2–3½ years) promoted through parent groups and a baby programme (birth to 2 years) promoted largely by health visitors. The programme would normally be used with parents by professional organisers rather than being given to parents to work through on their own. Donachy has produced a 'Guide for Professional Users' and a 'Commentary on the Guide' giving the rationale, which would be of assistance to professionals setting up groups. Since the emphasis is on ordinary everyday activities using materials likely to be readily available in homes, these are programmes that might have a wide application without involving great expense.

A similar intervention was carried out in Cradley in England (Rathbone and Wheldall, 1979). Again the emphasis was on the provision of books for reading at home and a programme of language stimulation using common activities and games. It was found that 'significantly greater gains in both vocabulary and sentence comprehension scores were achieved by the children whose parents were involved in the programme'. The low cost of setting up such a programme was also pointed out.

GETTING STARTED

The main lesson to be learnt from all initiatives in parental involvement is the need for planning. Partnership with parents does not just happen, it involves a great deal of hard work and commitment. The first step in any intervention is to examine the current situation. Questions should be asked about both sides of the partnership.

Parents

Look around the nursery every half hour each day for two weeks. Note which parents are present and what they are doing.

What motivates these parents to come?

Why do others not come?

What attempts have been made to reach parents who do not come? Rheubottom (1983) discusses the problems of involving parents whose children are transported to nursery by taxi from some distance away.

Do any parents have obvious skills which could be useful in encouraging and organising other parents?

Staff

What are the attitudes of individual staff members towards parents?

Do parents seem to relate well to a particular member of staff?

Do any members of staff have training or experience in group work or counselling?

What can be done to develop these skills in staff?

Can any other professionals help?

Obviously there are many more factors to be examined but these are the sorts of questions that need to be answered. Mittler (1987) provides an extensive list of suggestions for staff wishing to develop parental involvement.

The initial steps need not be elaborate or require a great deal of investment in scarce resources. Pinkerton carried out a short study in a day nursery in which there was a great deal of daily contact between staff and parents but poor communication (Hughes *et al.*, 1980). Conversations rarely centred on the children and staff felt that the parents were really not interested. Parents, however, felt that staff were too busy and there was no time to discuss individual problems. Pinkerton provided some simple channels of communication, such as the showing of a relevant video tape, written information about nursery activities and lists of suitable reading material for parents and children. 'Parental interest in these things was overwhelming and, as a result, the staff's preconceptions about the parents' lack of interest was quite dispelled' (Gipps, 1982b).

Parental involvement is a complex issue in pre-school education. If three factors can be highlighted as being of paramount importance, they would be the following.

Firstly, staff must have a genuine commitment to working with parents. This requires not only positive attitudes but also the skills and confidence necessary to work with parents individually and in groups. As Watt (1983) points out, 'there is an outstanding need for inservice structures which support and encourage teachers in their role within the community at large'.

Secondly, staff must be sensitive to the needs of individual parents and their families. These needs change frequently over the course of time, especially when parents are coming to terms with the implications of their child's special needs.

Finally, as Watt and Flett (1985) recommended, 'we live in an age when the written word carries authority and credibility. If parental involvement [is an] important concept in early education it is important that [it] should be given status in written regional statements in the same way as other aspects of the curriculum.'

The integrated nursery in operation: policy and organisation

Many aspects of pre-school education for children with special needs have been discussed, with the emphasis on what happens within the nursery. Roles and responsibilities have been examined by focusing on children, parents, staff and other professionals. Activities in the nursery have been discussed by considering curriculum, learning, play and interaction. The need for assessment, monitoring and record keeping has been stressed.

This final chapter will focus on wider issues by examining the organisation and management of pre-school education for children with special needs. The need for clear policies on admission of children and placement after nursery will be stressed. An overview of a child's experiences from birth to 5 years will alert the reader to the many possible 'transitions' involved before school and the need to limit the range of pre-school experiences for individual children.

Finally, the place of the nursery within the wider community will be considered in terms of the community school movement, whereby the nursery would meet the wider needs of the community, not just the needs of pre-school children.

COMBINED NURSERY CENTRES

It is only realistic to assume that, for the next few years, nursery education will be provided largely in nursery schools and classes with day care continuing to be provided by day nurseries. Arguments have been presented throughout this book for the expansion of combined nursery centres and it is envisaged that this will be the future pattern of pre-school provision. The integration of children with special needs demands greater flexibility than is found within traditional nursery education. Nursery centres would be able to offer an extended day, physical care and provision for a wider age range throughout 52 weeks of the year. While most children would probably attend part-time during school terms for one or two years, some children with special needs would benefit from extended provision. Children from disadvantaged home circumstances, currently within the remit of day nurseries, are obvious examples but so, too, are children with developmental delay and learning difficulties who make good progress during term then often regress during long holiday periods. Some attendance at nursery during the summer vacation would help to consolidate new skills and maintain progress.

DESIGNATED NURSERIES TO MEET SPECIAL NEEDS

All nurseries can expect to find more children with special needs in attendance. It is unrealistic and uneconomical, however, to expect every nursery to be able to meet every need. Some children require sophisticated and expensive resources, others may require the skills of highly trained and scarce personnel. It is advocated, therefore, that some nurseries be provided with extra resources to meet specific needs, as the following examples illustrate.

Provision for hearing-impaired children in the ordinary nursery has set the pattern for integrated units. A special class is set up within the ordinary nursery to provide the equipment and materials necessary for hearing-impaired children. A specialist teacher is appointed and works with the children in small groups or individually, but a large part of the child's play is spent with ordinary children in the nursery. The needs of visually impaired children and those with severe language disorders could also be met within this pattern of provision. The units can act as resource centres for other nurseries in the area and the specialist teacher may be able to provide some assistance to staff in other nurseries on a peripatetic basis.

Some nurseries will never be able to accept children with severe physical disabilities because of lack of space or limitations created by the design of the building. Many nurseries could readily be adapted with a few minor alterations. Obvious adaptations would relate to access, doors, toilet facilities and general mobility. Some of these factors were discussed in Chapter 5. Modern building design and planning now take more account of the needs of the disabled and it is hoped that all new nurseries will be fully accessible.

Designating certain nurseries to cater for specific needs raises two important points. Firstly, in seeking to place a child in a particular nursery it must be ensured that the placement is fully acceptable from the point of view of the child *and* of the nursery. It is important that a balance is maintained in the nursery so that the needs of some children do not overshadow the needs of others. If staff in a nursery are asked to cope with too many children with special needs, the provision ceases to be 'ordinary', the benefits of integration are lost and children with no special needs can be overlooked. The suggestion that one child in every ten attending an ordinary nursery should have special needs has been made in recent years but this is not a very realistic or useful guideline because of the diversity of special needs. The needs of a child with a specific language disorder cannot be equated with the needs of a child with spina bifida, which in turn are very different from the needs of a hearing-impaired child. Many 'ordinary' children will have special needs at times. Specific ratios of special needs children to ordinary children should not be considered. All those involved in the placement of children should have a thorough knowledge of each nursery and be sensitive to the balance that must be maintained. The final decision regarding the admission of a particular child should rest with the nursery staff.

Secondly, if some nurseries are designated to meet particular needs, children will travel to nursery from some distance away. Transport will be provided but special efforts will have to be made to ensure that the children and their families receive the full benefits of nursery placement. Rheubottom (1983) carried out a survey of parents whose children went to school by taxi and found two main areas of concern. Children were being singled out as different if they travelled by taxi, not only among their friends at school but also within the family, where brothers and sisters travelled to school in the normal way, sometimes even to the same school. This detracted from their experience of integration. Perhaps more seriously, parents lost the benefits of regular informal contact with staff and other parents, which normally comes about when children are taken to nursery and collected in the normal way. Staff must make special arrangements to ensure that communication with home is not lost, perhaps by arranging home/school diaries, newsletters, regular parents' days and workshops, as well as home visits by nursery staff.

RELATIONSHIPS WITH NURSERY CLASSES IN SPECIAL SCHOOLS

Just as integrated special units can be used as resource centres, so special nurseries should also be closely linked with ordinary provision. There will always be a need for special nurseries to cater for children with severe and multiple handicaps, for those who are too delicate to cope with the ordinary nursery environment and for those for whom there is no suitable alternative provision in the area. Special school staff should have an important role to play in the inservice training of ordinary nursery staff by coming into the nurseries to talk to staff and by inviting nursery staff into the special school to observe and learn.

Exchange visits should also be possible for children attending ordinary and special provision. A nursery school and special nursery class in Birmingham formed close links by organising such visits. Two children from the special class attended the ordinary nursery with one of their teachers for two mornings each week. Staff and children from the ordinary nursery visited the special school in the same way. It was found that with careful planning such visits could be of great benefit to all the children and staff involved.

RELATIONSHIPS WITH OTHER PROFESSIONALS

As well as drawing on the support and expertise of specialist teachers, nursery staff must establish clear links with other professionals to ensure the practice of 'united responsibility' for special needs as discussed in Chapter 6. Various professional agencies and roles were identified and it was suggested that a 'named person' might act as the co-ordinator and facilitator of action in connection with a particular child. The relationship between staff and other professionals must not, however, depend on casework alone but should be based on explicit guidelines within a policy of united responsibility. For example, each large nursery centre should have the services of a social worker who visits the nursery regularly, preferably at particular times that are known to staff and parents.

Similarly, an educational psychologist with interest and expertise in pre-school education should be attached to the nursery, visiting regularly to discuss general matters of curriculum and assessment and take part in inservice training, as well as carrying out casework.

It is important that one professional from each agency has the main responsibility for children in the nursery so that a thorough knowledge of the nursery can be acquired and relationships can be developed with staff, children and parents. This social worker or psychologist should take responsibility for all children on admission to the nursery. Social workers and psychologists who have been involved with children who live some distance away and who are likely to become involved again when the children leave nursery, perhaps returning to school in their own neighbourhoods, should receive copies of reports and be invited to attend case discussions and conferences.

Social workers and educational psychologists have been singled out to illustrate the relationship between nursery staff and other professionals. Health personnel, in particular health visitors, clinical psychologists and speech therapists, must have equally explicit lines of communication with nursery staff.

ADMISSIONS POLICY

The designation of particular nurseries for particular special needs and the involvement of a wide range of professional agencies in the identification of special needs and placement for pre-school children require that there must be a clear admissions policy and written guidelines outlining the functions and facilities offered by each nursery. Lindsay and Desforges (1986) report a study by Twistleton (1980), who found that 'key people involved in referring children had a very unclear idea about the units and the procedures by which children should be placed ... in the absence of guidance they resorted to individual practice and personal belief about how the units should operate.' Lindsay and Desforges (1986) stress that 'at the highest level there must be clear policy decisions by the LEA; when this clarity is missing, "street level" workers make their own "policy".'

A statement about the need for nursery staff to be furnished with background reports from relevant agencies at the earliest possible stage should be included in the admissions policy.

NURSERIES AS ASSESSMENT CENTRES

Chapter 6 was devoted to assessment in the pre-school years. Early identification of special needs is crucial so that intervention can begin without waste of time. Major developmental changes occur during the pre-school years and so continuous assessment and intervention must go hand in hand. It has been stressed that assessment is not something that is applied as step one, to be followed by remediation as step two.

This raises the question of the purpose of the short-term assessment centres which have been opening throughout the country. As Cash (1983) states, 'multi disciplinary child development centres were one of the last growth industries in the NHS. There are as many theories as to the role of these centres as there are people running them.' The concept of multi-disciplinary assessment is to be approved, but to place children with special needs in a segregated special nursery for a short period of time must have its limitations:

1. The child must become accustomed to new surroundings and to strange adults and children.

2. The high turnover of children means that friendships will be short-lived and must create feelings of insecurity in some children.
3. It is impossible to ascertain the extent to which a child could be integrated into an ordinary nursery.
4. Once assessment is complete, the child will then be removed to another nursery to begin adjusting all over again.

The development of integrated nursery centres for children with special needs should eliminate the need for assessing children in segregated, artificial settings. The nursery can become the focus of multi-disciplinary assessment. It provides a more natural environment and greater continuity and stability for the child. Undoubtedly it will be necessary to transfer some children to alternative provision if assessment reveals previously unknown difficulties or if a child's needs change, but for many children the original placement will be the correct one.

MANAGEMENT OF ABSENCES

Most nursery practitioners will have experience of children being absent from the nursery for an extended period of time because of illness or accident. An isolated case can be dealt with as it occurs. The integration of children with special needs requires that a more explicit policy be adopted regarding the management of prolonged or frequent absences. Some children require regular hospital treatment and operations, others are prone to illness and vulnerable to infections.

It is important that nursery staff maintain contact with a family whose child is in hospital or confined to home. Hospitals have become much more relaxed and informal in their provision for young children. As well as providing medical attention, they recognise the need to stimulate the children and keep them occupied, and play leaders and therapists are now found in many children's wards. If a child has been following a programme in nursery and is well enough, a nursery nurse or teacher might be able to liaise with a play leader so that the programme can continue in hospital. Similarly, a child can be visited at home by a member of the nursery staff, who can give parents ideas on ways to stimulate and occupy the child who is confined. Other parents might be able to visit to bring news from the nursery. Anything that can be done to continue the child's education and prevent the parents from feeling isolated and cut off from support will be beneficial and make the return to nursery easier.

The child's return to nursery must be planned and carefully managed. Requirements will depend on the length of a child's absence and on health factors and it may be that re-entry should be gradual, beginning with part-time attendance.

MOVING ON

The transition from pre-school into school has attracted a great deal of professional and media interest in recent years. Two main topics of debate can be identified and are to some extent overlapping. One concerns continuity in early education and the relationship between the nursery experience and the reception class experience for a child. The other concerns the age at which children should enter reception classes.

Continuity with extension

The relationship between nursery and primary education has become closer during the past two decades and the boundaries are becoming less distinct. Watt (1987) suggests two possible reasons for this. Firstly, the nursery years have been recognised as vitally important in laying foundations for later learning. Nursery education can make a difference to a child's later academic performance but, as the Head Start programmes in the United States in the 1960s demonstrated, primary schools must make an effort to build on the pre-school experience if gains are not to be lost through discontinuity (Bereiter, 1972). Secondly, 'because at least in professional circles "early education" is taken to mean formal education of children aged 3 to 8 and most training courses cover that age-range, we can assume a professional commitment to continuity between the two stages' (Watt, 1987).

A major research project was carried out between 1977 and 1980, entitled *Continuity of Children's Experience in the Years Three to Eight* and funded by the DES (Cleave *et al.*, 1982; Cleave, 1982). The aims of the study were to examine the experiences of children in a wide range of pre-school facilities and the infant school and to focus on a group of children around the time of transfer to infant school. A great many areas of potential discontinuity of experience were identified and a wealth of practical suggestions was provided for helping children to cope with the new situation. Children need compatibility and stimulation but not total 'shock', the ideal situation being described as 'continuity with extension'. The researchers looked closely at the setting, the curriculum, the people, personal relationships and the family. There is no space here to describe all the coping strategies that are given and the reader is recommended to refer to the original sources. A summary of the advice given to cope with the new people in the infant school will be given to illustrate the kinds of strategies suggested.

Critical features

1. Contact with crowds of children who are older, bigger and noisier than himself.
2. The presence of few or unfamiliar adults away from the classroom, particularly in the playground and at dinner.
3. Organisational procedures which may necessitate lining-up, queueing and waiting.
4. Competition for adult attention.
5. Being addressed as one of a group or class.
6. Restrictions on movement and noise and on opportunities for interaction with other children.
7. Organisational constraints on time, with the possibility of being last or left behind.

Strategies to minimise the effects of discontinuity

1. Keeping the reception class intact and separate at first to allow new entrants to get to know their classmates.
2. Allowing new entrants to arrive and leave school at a different time from the rest to avoid the crush.
3. Introducing new entrants gradually to mass events outside the classroom.
4. Allowing new entrants access to siblings and friends, especially at playtime.
5. Providing corners into which new entrants can withdraw.
6. Having the reception teacher present in new situations, such as assembly.
7. Giving the child pre-school experience of being part of a formal group.
8. Making use of auxiliary helpers, such as parents and older children, so that new entrants are not left behind.

This study found that parents had only minimal involvement in their child's transition from nursery into school. This must cause some concern, particularly in the light of the finding from another study (Watt and Flett, 1985) that:

> continuity in education is achieved only to the extent that parents are involved in the educational process since it is they who provide the continuing long-term influence in the wider context of the child's life.
>
> Watt (1987)

In view of the increasing attention given to parental involvement, as discussed in the last chapter, it is crucial that parents should not be excluded from this important stage.

Watt and Flett (1985) raised two other relevant concerns. Firstly, they found a lack of any written record being passed from nursery to infant school, which they attribute to the prevalent attitude that children should start school with a 'clean slate.' This is consistent with the findings of Clark *et al.* (1982). It hardly needs to be stated that this is a serious error, particularly in the case of children with special needs. It has been stated frequently throughout this book that assessment, record keeping and monitoring of progress are essential and continuity into school cannot possibly be achieved if infant teachers are oblivious to all that has been done before. Some children will have statements, under the requirements of the Education Act 1981, that will be transferred with them but they, and many others, will require more detailed record cards and notes to be passed on.

Secondly, most nursery schools send children to a variety of primary schools and many nursery classes also send children to several schools other than the school to which they are attached. The dispersal of children with special needs is likely to be even wider, some going to special schools and special units within ordinary schools. Considerable effort must be made to link with a child's future school so that visits and other preparations can be made before entry. The child and parents should obviously visit the school on several occasions. It is also important that prospective infant class teachers should visit the nursery to see the child there and observe nursery staff working with the child.

Age on entering school

> Evidence from other countries ... suggests that the statutory age of admission to school in the United Kingdom is already amongst the lowest in Europe and in the United States of America. Research findings by the National Foundation for Educational Research (NFER) demonstrate that there is a trend in England and Wales towards admitting children to school at a younger age. Data provided by 90 local education authorities in 1986 show that the annual admission at the beginning of the school year of the child's fifth birthday has become the predominant mode of entry to school .... Current provision for young children in infant classes appears to fall short of that recommended by a recent Parliamentary Select Committee, particularly with reference to class size and ancillary support.
>
> Sharp (1988)

This extract is taken from the abstract of a research report entitled *Starting School at Four* and sums up the main reasons for concern in the current debate about age of school entry. The fact that children start school at a very early age in this country, the belief that this age is being gradually lowered further and the unsuitability of many infant classes for 4-year-olds have aroused considerable interest in recent years (Sewell, 1986; Bennett, 1987; Bayliss, 1988). Many contributions to this debate accuse local authorities of admitting younger children to school for political and administrative reasons rather than considering the best interests of the children. These reasons include raising numbers in infant schools to attract extra resources, reducing numbers in nurseries to justify cutting resources and finding it administratively useful to have a single intake of children at one point in the school year. The issue of school entry age is a highly complex one and cannot be fully discussed here. The reader is referred to Sharp (1988) for an up-to-date and thorough analysis of the situation.

A plea is made here for flexibility in the age of admission of children with special needs to ordinary school. Some children with special needs take longer to acquire new skills and their all-round development might be delayed. Transfer to school too soon might lead to failure, whereas an extra year in nursery might bring the child to a level of maturity that would ease the transition into school and increase the likelihood of successful integration. It is not suggested that children should be kept out of school beyond the age of 5 years but it would certainly seem inadvisable for a child with special needs to enter school at the age of 4.

ALTERNATIVE PROVISION

Private pre-schooling is a growth industry in the 1980s. Largely in response to lack of local authority provision, private nurseries are opening throughout the country, particularly in prosperous city and suburban areas (Wilce, 1987). In Lothian Region in Scotland the number of private nurseries has doubled in the past two years (Flowers, 1988).

Some of these private nurseries provide education but many are day care centres. This distinction is not always made explicit in nursery brochures and parents are often unaware of the differences. It is important that parents of children with special needs should choose a nursery where staff are trained and experienced in teaching such children. For example, a 3-year-old child with cerebral palsy was placed in a private nursery to give him two years' pre-school experience and to prepare him for ordinary school. His parents then referred the child to an educational psychologist for assessment and advice. The psychologist discovered that the nursery owner had no relevant pre-school experience and ran the nursery as a business venture. The staff comprised two nursery nurses who were recently qualified and two unqualified women under the age of 20. The nursery regime was satisfactory and the staff were caring and willing but they had no training or experience with children with special needs and this child had very complex learning difficulties and mobility problems. The parents had thought that this was a nursery school and that the child would receive the attention of qualified teachers. Transfer to another nursery had to be recommended and was very disruptive for the child.

RESTRICT PRE-SCHOOL EXPERIENCES

This may seem a strange suggestion to come at the end of a book that has argued for the expansion of nursery provision and maximisation of a child's potential in the pre-school years, but it is a very important issue.

It is not uncommon for a small child, after a few months spent in the home, to attend a mother and toddler group. This may be followed, depending on local provision, by a year in a playgroup, then a year in a nursery school or class, then entry into school. The whole question of transition into school fades into insignificance, since the children have had to become experts at transition, having experienced three major changes in four years (and possibly more if the family have moved house to another area during that time). Imagine how stressful it would be for an adult to change employment three times in four years! Certainly, some of the children will remain the same at each stage but the environment, the adults and the regime will be very different. Watt and Flett (1985) were concerned that the pre-school children in their study did not spend an extended period of time in any one group. This has a disruptive influence on the child, and makes it impossible for staff to get to know a child well. Thus problems may pass unnoticed.

Obviously, this situation is untenable for a child with special needs. As soon as a child's needs have been identified, it is strongly suggested that the pre-school years are fully planned so that the child receives maximum assistance with the minimum of disruption and discontinuity. Future assessment or a change in the child's needs might require that this plan be altered, but at least attention will have been drawn to the need for stability, security and continuity.

REVOLUTIONS!

There is an air of excitement in pre-school education at the present time. Following years of inactivity and retrograde steps, as outlined in our historical overview, there are indications that sweeping changes will take place in pre-school provision before the end of the century. The two major integration revolutions are already underway. Combined nursery centres will weather the storms of organisational and staffing difficulties to provide integrated services for the under-fives with no artificial distinction between their care and their education. This new framework for pre-school education will mean that many more children with special needs can attend ordinary nurseries. All that remains is for the government to build on the foundations that have been laid by providing the resources necessary to allow ordinary pre-school education to meet a wide range of special educational needs.

> Statements of needs will undoubtedly highlight the shortage of specialist teachers, physiotherapists, speech therapists, educational psychologists, nurses and doctors. Those in a position to alter policy should be prepared to meet these special needs; after all, they have set up a statutory framework to identify them.
>
> Cash (1983)

Appendix 1 Manual of observation schedule for use in pre-school units

A. INTERACTION CATEGORIES

	+	+	+	−	−	−	0	
INI	V	M	NV	V	M	NV		Insert 'C' 'P' or 'T'
RES	1	2	3	4	5	6	7	

+V: *Positive verbal.* A remark from one person to another which is friendly and non-threatening.

+NV: *Positive non-verbal.* (a) Physical contact which is friendly and non-hostile. Includes cuddling, taking hands, patting, stroking, touching an object which another is holding. (b) Carrying out an instruction, obeying a request.

−V: *Negative verbal.* A remark from one person to another which is hostile, threatening, aggressive.

−NV: *Negative non-verbal.* (a) Physical contact which is hostile, threatening, aggressive. Includes pushing, hitting, snatching toy from another against his wishes, destroying something another is building. (b) Refusing to carry out an instruction or obey a request, e.g. shaking head, running away, turning away.

M: *Mixed verbal/non-verbal.* Physical contact plus simultaneous verbalisation.

0: *No interaction has occurred.*

INI: *Initiation.* Record of the person who made the first move in the interaction (see C, P and T below).

RES: *Response.* Record of the person who responded or made the second move in the interaction.

C. Child being observed.

P. Peer, any other child.

T. Teacher, nurse, any other adult.

B. CATEGORIES OF ACTIVITY

Fc	Fs	GA	GM	IP	B	SG	LW		NS
1	2	3	4	5	6	7	8		14

1 Fc: Fine perceptual-motor (creative). Unstructured fine perceptual-motor activity: no rigid rules; no right/wrong distinction.
Includes modelling, painting, drawing, Lego, small construction,
stringing beads, some sand and water play, craft activities, some
cutting, gluing, carpentry.
2 Fs: Fine perceptual-motor (structured). Fine perceptual-motor
activity with rigid rules and goals; clear right/wrong distinction,
since there are limited number of acceptable outcomes. Includes
jigsaws, table games (picture bingo, snakes and ladders, ludo,
etc.), cutting shapes, putting on/taking off clothes.
3 GA: Gross physical activity. Movement over the ground without
use of toys or other equipment. Includes running, jumping,
hopping and walking. Location will always be solitary or parallel
or group or teacher – if children are involved in GA in association,
then SG is recorded (see below).
4 GM: Gross perceptual-motor. Gross movement involving equipment or toys. Includes climbing frame, swings, vehicles, chute.
Location recorded as with GA.
5 IP: Imaginative play. Child is involved in fantasy; has adopted
role of particular person and is acting the part, e.g. Superman,
policeman, nurse *or* is pretending that an object represents
something else, e.g. child uses cutlery to 'shoot' as if it were a
gun.
6 B: Book/story activity. Child is (a) listening to a story being
read, (b) 'reading' by him/herself – includes books, comics, wall
posters, (c) listening to a story on record, tape or television.
7 SG: Small group activity. Two or more children involved in
association without the controlling presence of an adult. Includes
rough and tumble play, peek-a-boo, hide and seek, gross physical
and perceptual-motor play in association. If an adult has set up
the activity and is absent for a few minutes this is not recorded as
SG, since adult control is present – the group must be a
spontaneous one set up by the children.
8 LW: Looking, listening, waiting. The child is inactive and is
looking or listening to others, waiting for equipment to arrive, or
an activity to begin. Location is recorded as solitary or group
(when child is sitting in group but is not involved in what the
group is doing). Parallel, association and teacher cannot be
recorded.

Blank box for one of five activities to be recorded by initial:

9   *M: Music/dancing*. (a) Listening to music on tape, record, television, piano, (b) participating in songs, dancing, movement to music, singing games.

10   *H: Helping an adult*. To organise, fetch and tidy away equipment.

11   *T: Toilet/washing activities*. Includes going to the toilet area, using toilet, sink or mirror, queueing to leave toilet area.

12   *S: Snacks*. Includes waiting for the snack to be served, and eating and drinking.

13   *C: Conversing*. Child is talking to adult or peer and *doing nothing else*. If he or she is involved in another activity at the same time, record the other activity only. Location for 'C' is always association or teacher.

14   *NS: Non-specific activity*. Child is wandering aimlessly, not involved in any activity which could be included in the above categories.

C. LOCATION CATEGORIES

S	P	A	G	T
1	2	3	4	5

S: Solitary play. Child is engaged in activity alone. No child within conversation distance is engaged in the same activity.

P: Parallel play. Child is engaged in activity alongside other child/children. The other(s) must be engaged in the same activity. They work independently and without roles.

A: Associative play. Child is engaged in activity *with* other child/children. Roles are taken, the boundary of the group is clearly defined, the presence of the other(s) is necessary for the activity to continue.

G: Group activity. Child is involved in formal group activity organised and controlled by adult. The child's participation can be voluntary or compulsory.

T: Teacher/adult. Child is engaged in activity in parallel or association with an adult. No peers are present. If one or more peer is present and engaged in the same activity, 'G' is recorded.

OBSERVATION PROCEDURE

1. *Complete information* on the front observation sheet – unit, child's name, date and your initials. Leave code blank.

2. *Locate child* and start stopwatch. Observe for one minute without recording in order to tune into the child's activity.
3. Begin 20-minute observation session. You will complete one observation of interaction, activity and location *every 30 seconds* as follows:
   Observe for 20 seconds. Mentally note activity and location in the first second then wait for the first interaction involving target child to occur. When it occurs, observe who initiated, who responded and whether it was verbal/non-verbal and positive/negative. Immediately complete the first block on schedule:
   (a) *Interaction*: 'C', 'P' or 'T' in the appropriate box on the top line for initiation and 'C', 'P' or 'T' on the bottom line for response.
   (b) *Activity*: Circle the number below the appropriate category or place the appropriate initial in the blank box.
   (c) *Location*: Circle the number of the appropriate category.
   If no interaction occurs during the 20 seconds' observation, record activity and location only. If an interaction is clearly initiated but there is no response, record the initiation in the usual way and put 'C', 'P' or 'T' in response box 7 to indicate who did not respond.
   You have 10 seconds to record before the next observation period begins.
4. Observe and record continuously for 20 minutes, completing 40 blocks on the observation sheets. Work down the columns of the observation sheets, *not* across the rows.

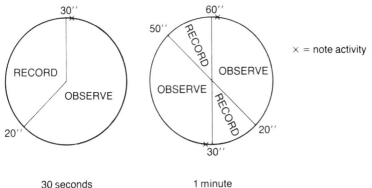

| 30 seconds | 1 minute |

Note
If an interaction is already ongoing at the beginning of a 20-second observation period, place a large cross at the side of the interaction grid. If that interaction ends and another begins before the end of the 20-second period, record the new interaction as well as the cross.

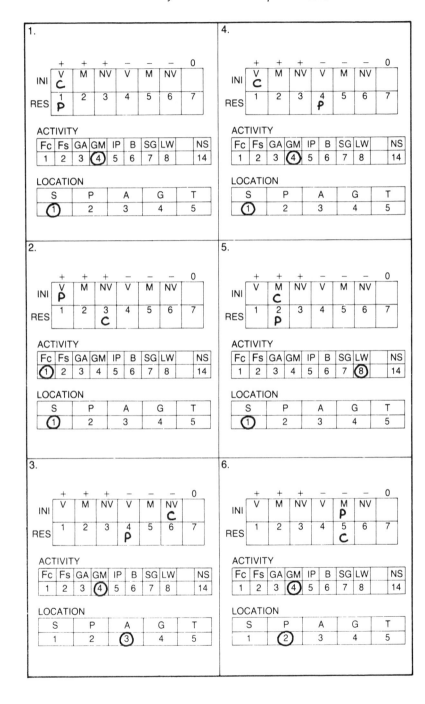

7.

	+ V	+ M	+ NV	− V	− M	− NV	0
INI		P					
RES	1	2	3	4	5	6 C	7

ACTIVITY

Fc	Fs	GA	GM	IP	B	SG	LW		NS
1	2	3	4	⑤	6	7	8		14

LOCATION

S	P	A	G	T
1	2	③	4	5

10.

	+ V	+ M	+ NV	− V	− M	− NV	0
INI	T						
RES	1	2	3	4	5	6	7 C

ACTIVITY

Fc	Fs	GA	GM	IP	B	SG	LW		NS
①	2	3	4	5	6	7	8		14

LOCATION

S	P	A	G	T
1	2	3	④	5

8.

	+ V	+ M	+ NV	− V	− M	− NV	0
INI						C	
RES	1	2	3	4	5	6	7 P

ACTIVITY

Fc	Fs	GA	GM	IP	B	SG	LW		NS
1	2	3	4	5	6	7	8		⑭

LOCATION

S	P	A	G	T
①	2	3	4	5

11.

	+ V	+ M	+ NV	− V	− M	− NV	0
INI			P				
RES	1	2	3	4	5	6 C	7

ACTIVITY

Fc	Fs	GA	GM	IP	B	SG	LW		NS
1	2	3	4	5	⑥	7	8		14

LOCATION

S	P	A	G	T
1	②	3	4	5

9.

	+ V	+ M	+ NV	− V	− M	− NV	0
INI	C						
RES	1	2	3	4	5	6	7 T

ACTIVITY

Fc	Fs	GA	GM	IP	B	SG	LW		NS
1	2	3	4	5	6	7	⑧		14

LOCATION

S	P	A	G	T
①	2	3	4	5

12.

	+ V	+ M	+ NV	− V	− M	− NV	0
INI		T					
RES	1	2 C	3	4	5	6	7

ACTIVITY

Fc	Fs	GA	GM	IP	B	SG	LW		NS
①	2	3	4	5	6	7	8		14

LOCATION

S	P	A	G	T
1	2	3	④	5

EXAMPLES OF RECORD SHEET COMPLETION

Examples of possible recordings are shown on pages 152 and 153 (actual score sheets contained 15 grids). The activity and location are self-explanatory. Notes on interaction are provided below, using examples of interaction recorded in a large nursery school.

1. Target child initiates positive verbal interaction. Peer gives positive verbal response.
   C: Would you like to play with me?
   P: Yes, when I take my coat off.
   C: Would you like to play with me?
   P: No, not now but after storytime.
2. Peer initiates positive verbal interaction. Target child gives positive non-verbal response.
   P: I want to wash my hands.
   C: [*Takes his hand and leads him to the sink*]
3. Target child initiates negative non-verbal interaction. Peer gives negative verbal response.
   C: [*Pushes peer roughly out of the way*]
   P: Don't you do that again or I'll kick you!
   C: [*Snatches doll from peer*]
   P: That's mine – give me it!
4. Target child initiates positive verbal interaction. Peer gives negative verbal response.
   C: I'd like to kick the ball too.
   P: Well you can't because you're not playing with us!
5. Target child initiates positive verbal interaction accompanied by positive physical contact. Peer responds likewise.
   C: Are you my friend? [*putting her arm around other child's shoulder*]
   P: Yes, we're friends. [*putting his arm around child's waist*]
6. Peer initiates negative verbal interaction accompanied by negative physical contact. Target child responds likewise.
   P: I want to play with that scooter! [*pushing child off scooter*]
   C: No, I had it first! [*hitting peer*]
7. Peer initiates positive verbal interaction accompanied by positive physical contact. Child responds with negative action.
   P: Would you like to have the red dress for your doll? [*placing dress in child's hand*]
   C: [*Throws dress on the floor and runs off*]

8. Child initiates negative non-verbal interaction. There is no response.
   [*Child approaches peer and kicks over brick tower. Peer does nothing.*
   Child pushes over peer. Peer starts to cry but does not respond.
   Crying is a reaction but it is not a response in terms of interaction.]
9. Child initiates positive verbal interaction. There is no response.
   C: Can I go outside please?
   T: [*Continues to wash paintbrushes and does not respond*]
10. Teacher makes positive statement to child which child ignores.
   T: James, will you come and have your milk now?
   C: [*Continues to paint and does not respond*]
11. Peer initiates positive non-verbal interaction. Child's response is negative non-verbal.
   P: [*Comes across and puts arm around child's shoulder*]
   C: [*Pushes peer away and walks off*]
12. Teacher initiates positive verbal interaction accompanied by positive physical contact. Child responds likewise.
   T: That's a beautiful snowman, let me fix its buttons.
       [*Takes the snowman which the child is holding, fixes the buttons then holds it out to the child*]
   C: That's better. Can I put on the scarf now? [*Child takes the snowman from the teacher*]

Appendix 2 Play resources

ADDRESSES

Toys for the Handicapped
76 Barracks Road
Sandy Lane Industrial Estate
Stourport-on-Severn
Worcestershire
DY13 9QB

Handicapped Persons Research Unit
Newcastle Polytechnic
Coach Lane Campus
Newcastle upon Tyne

Toy Aids Project
Lodbourne Farmhouse
Lodbourne Green
Gillingham
Dorset

Toy Libraries Association
Seabrook House
Wyllyoths Manor
Darkes Lane
Potters Bar
Hertfordshire

Play-Aid Supplies Ltd
Shanval Estate
South Road
Temple Fields
Harlow
Essex

Hester Hope Ltd
St Philips Drive
Royton
Oldham
OL2 6AG

The Spastics Society
16 Fitzroy Square
London
W1N 5HQ

Bradford Activity Toys
103 Dockfield Road
Shipley
West Yorkshire
BD17 7AR

Relyon
Hospitals Division
Wellington
Somerset

National Centre for Play
Moray House College of Education
Holyrood Campus
Edinburgh

USEFUL REFERENCES

Arnheim, D. D. and Sinclair, W. A. (1975) *The Clumsy Child*. C. V. Mosby.

Carden, W. (1985) *Anson House Preschool Project, 5. Special Toys*. Barkingside: Barnardo's.

Cass, J. (1971) *The Significance of Children's Play*. London: Batsford.

Lear, R. (1977) *Play Helps*. London: Heinemann.

McLean, E. (1983) 'Playing together: running an integrated play-scheme – and living to tell the tale!' *Mental Handicap*, **11**, pp. 156–158.

Matterson, E. M. (1975) *Play with a Purpose for the Under 7s*. Harmondsworth: Penguin.

Murphy, L. (1978) *Before School*. London: Cassell.

Newson, J. and Newson, E. (1979) *Toys and Playthings*. London: George Allen and Unwin.

Richardson, A. M., Reid, G., Phemister, M. R. and Thomas, G. V.

(1981) 'Play materials for mentally handicapped children'. *Child: Care, Health and Development*, **7**, pp. 317–329.

Riddick, B. (1982) *Toys and Play for the Handicapped Child*. Beckenham: Croom Helm.

Warren, R. (1986) *Special Needs – Pre-School Play*. Edinburgh: National Centre for Play.

Appendix 3 Glossary

asthma: in an attack of asthma breathing becomes difficult, expiration often being more affected than inspiration. The child is short of breath and 'wheezy', with coughing. The attack may be short, lasting for a few minutes, or very long, after which the child may be exhausted. Asthma is caused by numerous factors, including allergy, physical or chemical irritants, lung infections, prolonged exertion or emotional problems.

autism: childhood autism can be defined by the presence of language impairments, poverty of social interaction and repetitive stereotyped activities (see Howlin, P. and Rutter, M. (1987) *Treatment of Autistic Children*. Chichester: Wiley).

Batten's Disease: a degenerative condition which affects many areas of bodily function, including vision, locomotion and mental ability.

central deafness: an auditory processing disorder. The person seems to sense the signal adequately but is unable to process it. Also called auditory agnosia, word deafness and receptive aphasia.

cerebral palsy: in the cerebral palsies, physical handicap results directly from brain abnormality. Children may suffer from spasticity, which is muscular rigidity and partial paralysis, described as hemiplegia, diplegia and quadriplegia, depending on the number of limbs affected. Cerebral palsy may also be accompanied by ataxia (awkwardness of movement) and dyskinesia (including athetosis, involuntary movement).

cleft palate: hare lip and cleft palate are congenital splits of the lips and roof of the mouth which are corrected by surgery.

club-foot: a congenital deformity which prevents the foot being placed flat on the ground. The main defect may be in the heel, which is pulled upward and inward so that the child walks on his or her toes. Alternatively the toes are pulled back and the child walks on his or her heels. The foot itself may be twisted so that only the outer or inner edge touches the floor.

concrete operations: a Piagetian 'stage' of development from 18 months to 11 years approximately, divided into the preoperational period until the age of 7, followed by the period of concrete operations.

DES: Department of Education and Science.

Down's Syndrome: a congenital disorder consisting of moderate to severe learning difficulties accompanied by physical abnormalities (see Chapter 2).

dysphasia: expressive dysphasia refers to any disturbance in speech production. Receptive dysphasia refers to any disturbance in the understanding of spoken language.

echolalia: the child 'echoes' or repeats what is said by others.

eczema: a reaction of the skin to a wide range of stimulants or irritants, some known, many unknown. It causes itching and redness of the skin with oozing sores.

EEG: electro-encephalography. In the brain there is a regular, rhythmical change of electric potential due to the rhythmic discharge of energy by nerve cells. These changes can be recorded graphically and the 'brainwaves' examined.

epilepsy: disorganised electrical activity in the brain leading to transient attacks of disturbed motor and sensory functions. Petit mal attacks may be difficult to recognise, especially in young children. The child may appear to be daydreaming for a few seconds. In grand mal attacks, the child will fall to the ground. Consciousness is lost and the muscles jerk violently.

grammar: a disorder of grammatic knowledge is one in which knowledge of the appropriate structures is impaired. There are many forms, including omission of verb inflections, misplacement of negatives, unconventional word order and incorrect use of morphemes.

hare lip: see cleft palate.

hydrocephalus: an abnormal accumulation of cerebrospinal fluid within the skull, indicated by enlarging of the head.

LEA: local education authority.

Leish–Nyhan Syndrome: a rare chemical disorder resulting in severe learning difficulties.

microcephalus: abnormal smallness of the head.

morpheme: refers to the smallest meaningful unit in a language, whether it is a word or a part of a word. Words are free morphemes. Prefixes and suffixes are bound morphemes.

phoneme: the phonemes of a language are the sounds that distinguish meaning in that language. In each language phonemes are combined according to rules. English is described phonetically by using 24 consonants and 15 simple vowel sounds.

pragmatics: pragmatics sees language as a social event carried out by human beings in particular communicative contexts. Language is influenced by the function it serves and the social context in which it occurs.

semantics: implies an association between words and grammatical structures and their meanings.

spina bifida: in spina bifida some of the spinal bones which normally cover and protect the delicate spinal cord fail to develop properly and the normal bony projections over the spine are divided. Several conditions are included in the term spina bifida and they may occur at any point from the back of the head to the lowest part of the spine. In spina bifida occulta and meningocele the spinal cord is not harmed and there is no muscular weakness. In spina bifida myelomeningocele, the spinal cord is damaged and results in varying degrees of paralysis and incontinence.

stammer: stammering or stuttering is a disturbance of speech in which it is abruptly interrupted or certain sounds or syllables are rapidly repeated.

syntax: is used to describe the manner in which the order of words can have grammatic significance.

References

Albutt, L. (1980) *Social Interactions of Handicapped and Non-handicapped Pre-School Children*. Unpublished MSc special study, Division of Education, Sheffield University.

Aplin, G. and Pugh, G. (1983) *Perspectives on Pre-School Home Visiting*. London: National Children's Bureau.

Ashby, G. F. (1978) 'Australia'. In Chazan, M. (ed.) *International Research in Early Childhood Education*. Slough: NFER.

Attwood, T. (1977) 'The Priory Parents' Workshop'. *Child: Care, Health and Development*, **3**, pp. 81–91.

Attwood, T. (1978) 'The Croydon workshop for the parents of pre-school mentally handicapped children'. *Child: Care, Health and Development*, **4**, pp. 79–97.

Bain, A. and Barnett, L. (1981) *The Design of a Day Care System in a Nursery Setting for Children Under Five*. London: Tavistock Institute.

Baker, M., Foley, M. F., Glynn, T. and McNaughton, S. (1983) 'The effect of adult proximity and serving style on pre-schoolers' language and eating behaviour'. *Educational Psychology*, **3**, pp. 137–148.

Barnes, E. B. (1979) 'Peer interaction between typical and special children in an integrated setting'. *Dissertation Abstracts International*, (v), **40**, p. 190-A.

Bate, M. and Smith, M. (1978) *Manual for Assessment in Nursery Education*. Windsor: NFER-Nelson.

Bate, M., Smith, M. and James, J. (1981) *Review of Tests and Assessments in Early Education (3–5 years)*. Windsor: NFER-Nelson.

Bayley, N. (1969) *Bayley Scales of Infant Development*. New York: The Psychological Corporation.

Bayliss, S. (1988) 'Four years old and off to a shaky start'. *Times Educational Supplement*, 29 April.

Bellman, M. and Cash, J. (1987) *The Schedule of Growing Skills*. Windsor: NFER-Nelson.

Bennett, D. (1987) *Four Year Olds in School: Policy and Practice*. Windsor: NFER-Nelson.

Bereiter, C. (1972) *Pre-School Programmes for the Disadvantaged*. Baltimore: Johns Hopkins University Press.

Bereiter, C. and Engelmann, S. (1966) *Teaching Disadvantaged Children in the Pre-School*. New Jersey: Prentice-Hall.

Bernal, M. E., Gibson, D. M., William, D. E. and Pesses, D. I. (1971) 'A device for automatic audio tape recording'. *Journal of Applied Behaviour Analysis*, **4**, pp. 151–156.

Beveridge, S. (1983) 'Developing partnership: The Anson House Preschool Project'. In Mittler, P. and McConachie, H. (eds) *Parents, Professionals and Mentally Handicapped People – Approaches to Partnership*. Beckenham: Croom Helm.

Beveridge, S., Flanagan, R., McConachie, H. and Sebba, J. (1982) *Parental Involvement in Anson House. Anson House Preschool Project Paper 3.* Barkingside: Barnardo's.

Blank, M. (1972) 'The treatment of personality variables in a pre-school cognitive program'. In Stanley, J. C. (ed.) *Pre-School Programs for the Disadvantaged*. Baltimore: Johns Hopkins University Press.

Blank, M. (1974) 'Pre-school and/or education'. In Tizard, B. (ed.) *Early Childhood Education*. Slough: NFER.

Blank, M. (1976) *Two Speak to Learn*. Hamilton College of Education.

Blank, M. (1985) 'Classroom discourse: the neglected topic of the topic'. In Clark, M. M. (ed.) *Helping Communication in Early Education*, Educational Review Occasional Publication No. 11. University of Birmingham.

Blank, M. and Franklin, E. (1980) 'Dialogue with pre-schoolers – a cognitively based system of assessment'. *Applied Psycholinguistics*, 1, pp. 127–150.

Blank, M., Rose, S. A. and Berlin, L. J. (1978) *Pre-School Language Assessment Instrument*. New York: Grune-Stratton.

Blank, M. and Solomon, F. (1969) 'How shall the disadvantaged be taught?' *Child Development*, 4, pp. 47–61.

Blatchford, P., Battle, S. and Mays, J. (1982) *The First Transition: Home to Pre-School*. Windsor: NFER-Nelson.

Blurton-Jones, N. (1972) *Ethological Studies of Child Behaviour*. Cambridge: Cambridge University Press.

Board of Education (1936) *Nursery Schools and Nursery Classes*. London: HMSO.

Booth, A. (1985) 'In-service training at the O.U.' In Sayer, J. and Jones, N. (eds) *Teacher Training and Special Educational Needs*. Beckenham: Croom Helm.

Booth, T. (1981) 'Demystifying integration'. In Swann, W. (ed.) *The Practice of Special Education*. Oxford: Blackwell.

Borke, H. (1983) 'Piaget's mountains revisited: changes in the egocentric landscape'. In Donaldson, M., Grieve, R. and Pratt, C. (eds) *Early Childhood Development and Education*. Oxford: Blackwell.

Bowlby, J. (1951) *Maternal Care and Mental Health*. Geneva: WHO.

Brierley, J. D. (1981) *A Future for Nursery Nursing*. National Nursery Examination Board.

Brown, G. and Yule, G. (1983) *Discourse Analysis*. Cambridge: Cambridge University Press.

Browning, M. M., Anderson, C. A., Bailey, I. J., Law, I. H., MacLeod, C. and Suckling, M. H. (1983) *Identifying the Needs of Profoundly Mentally Handicapped Children*. Glasgow: Jordanhill College of Education.

Bruner, J. S. (1966) *Toward a Theory of Instruction*. Cambridge, Mass: Harvard University Press.

Bruner, J. (1980) *Under Five in Britain*. London: Grant McIntyre.

Bruner, J. S. (1981) 'Representation and cognitive development'. In

Roberts, M. and Tamburrini, J. (eds) *Child Development 0–5*. Edinburgh: Holmes McDougall.

Bruner, J. S., Oliver, R. R. and Greenfield, P. M. *et al.* (1966) *Studies in Cognitive Growth*. New York: Wiley.

Cameron, A. (1988) 'Lifelong learning – but not for the educators'. *Times Educational Supplement (Scotland)*, 29 April.

Cameron, R. J. (1986) *Portage: Pre-schoolers, Parents and Professionals: 10 Years of Achievement in the U.K.* Windsor: NFER-Nelson.

Carmichael, E. (1987) 'Penn and the EIS'. *Times Educational Supplement (Scotland)*, 2 October.

Cash, J. (1983) 'Looking at the doctor's role'. *Special Education – Forward Trends*, **10**, pp. 31–32.

Cassasus, B. (1987) 'Exam nerves at kindergarten'. *Times Educational Supplement*, 27 November.

Cave, E. (1974) 'Provisions for the severely mentally handicapped young child'. In Tizard, J. (ed.) *Mental Retardation: Concepts of Education and Research*. London: Butterworths.

Cazden, C. B. (1983) 'Play with language and metalinguistic awareness: one dimension of language experience'. In Donaldson, M., Grieve, R. and Pratt, C. (eds) *Early Childhood Development and Education*. Oxford: Blackwell.

Central Statistical Office (1987) *Social Trends*, (v), 17. London: HMSO.

Chazan, M. (1978) *International Research in Early Childhood Education*. Slough: NFER.

Chazan, M. and Laing, A. (1982) *Children with Special Needs – The Early Years*. Milton Keynes: Open University Press.

Chazan, M., Laing, A. F., Shackleton Bailey, M. and Jones, G. (1980) *Some of Our Children*. Wells: Open Books.

Clark, E. A. (1976) 'Teacher attitudes towards integration of children with handicap'. *Education and Training of the Mentally Retarded*, **11**, pp. 333–335.

Clark, M. M. (1979) 'Developments in pre-school education and the role of research'. In Clark, M. M. and Cheyne, W. M. (eds) *Studies in Pre-School Education*. Sevenoaks: Hodder and Stoughton.

Clark, M. M. (1983a) 'Communication and the education of the pre-school child with special needs'. In Clark, M. M. (ed.) *Special Educational Needs and Children Under Five*, Educational Review Occasional Publication No. 9. University of Birmingham.

Clark, M. M. (1983b) 'Early education: issues and evidence'. In Clark, M. M. and Wade, B. (eds) *Early Childhood Education – Educational Review Special Issue 15*, **35**, pp. 113–120.

Clark, M. M. (1988) *Children Under Five: Educational Research and Evidence*. London: Gordon and Breach.

Clark, M. M. and Cheyne, W. M. (1979) *Studies in Pre-School Education*. Sevenoaks: Hodder & Stoughton.

Clark, M. M., Riach, J. and Cheyne, W. (1977) *Handicapped Children and Pre-School Education*. Glasgow: University of Strathclyde.

Clark, M. M., Robson, B. and Browning, M. (1982) *Pre-School Education and Children with Special Needs*. University of Birmingham.

Clarke, J. (1987) 'Special provision'. *Times Educational Supplement*, 2 October.

Cleave, S. (1982) 'Continuity from pre-school to infant school'. *Educational Research*, **24**, pp. 163–173.

Cleave, S., Jowett, S. and Bate, M. (1982) *And So to School: a Study of Continuity from Pre-School to Infant School*. Windsor: NFER-Nelson.

Clements, J. C., Smith, J., Spain, B. and Watkeys, J. (1982) A preliminary investigation on the use of the Portage system in day nursery settings. *Child: Care, Health and Development*, **8**, pp. 123–131.

Cohen, D. (1987) *The Development of Play*. Beckenham: Croom Helm.

Collis, S. (1988) 'Nursery nurses – role play'. *Times Educational Supplement (Scotland)*, 8 April.

Cooke, T. P., Apollini, T. and Cooke, S. A. (1977) Normal pre-school children as behavioural models for retarded peers. *Exceptional Children*, **43**, pp. 531–532.

Copley, M., Bishop, M. and Porter, J. (1986) *Portage: More than a Teaching Programme*. Windsor: NFER-Nelson.

Coulthard, M. and Brazil, D. (1981) 'Exchange structure'. In Coulthard, M. and Montgomery, M. (eds) *Studies in Discourse Analysis*. London: Routledge & Kegan Paul.

Coulthard, M. and Montgomery, M. (1981) *Studies in Discourse Analysis*. London: Routledge & Kegan Paul.

Crowe, B. (1973) *The Playgroup Movement*. London: George Allen and Unwin.

Cunningham, C. (1986) 'Early intervention – some findings from the Manchester Cohort of Children with Down's Syndrome'. In Copley, M., Bishop, M. and Porter, J. (eds) *Portage: More than a Teaching Programme*. Windsor: NFER-Nelson.

Cunningham, M. A. and Dixon, M. (1961) 'The study of the language of an autistic child'. *Journal of Child Psychology and Psychiatry*, **2**, pp. 193–202.

Curtis, A. M. (1986) *A Curriculum for the Pre-School Child: Learning to Learn*. Windsor: NFER-Nelson.

Curtis, A. and Blatchford, P. (1981) *Meeting the Needs of Socially Handicapped Children*. Windsor: NFER-Nelson.

Curtis, A. and Hill, S. (1978) *My World: a Handbook of Ideas*. Windsor: NFER-Nelson.

Daly, B., Addington, J., Kerfoot, S. and Sigston, A. (1985) *Portage: The Importance of Parents*. Windsor: NFER-Nelson.

Davis, M. (1984) 'Too special, too soon?' *Special Education: Forward Trends*, **11**, pp. 6–8.

Department of Education and Science (DES) (1967) *Children and Their Primary Schools (Plowden Report)*. London: HMSO.

Department of Education and Science (DES) (1968) *Parent/Teacher Relations in Primary Schools, Education Survey 5*. London: HMSO.

Department of Education and Science (DES) (1975) *Preschool Education and Care: Some Topics Requiring Research and Development Projects*. London: DES.

Department of Education and Science (DES) (1978) *Special Educational Needs (Warnock Report)*. London: HMSO.

Department of Education and Science (DES) and Department of Health and Social Security (DHSS) (1983) *Assessments and Statements of Special Needs (Circular 1/83)*. London: HMSO.

de Villiers, P. A. and de Villiers, J. G. (1979) *Early Language*. London: Fontana/Open Books.

Dewart, H. and Summers, S. (1988) *Pragmatic and Early Communication Profile*. Windsor: NFER-Nelson.

Dewhirst, W. (1985) 'Settings as contexts for dialogue: guidelines for practice in the management and organisation of communication between children'. In Clark, M. M. (ed.) *Helping Communication in Early Education*, Educational Review Occasional Publication No. 11. University of Birmingham.

Dixon, A. (1987) 'First and four-most'. *Forum*, **30**, pp. 12–13.

Donachy, W. (1976) 'Parent participation in pre-school education'. *British Journal of Educational Psychology*, **46**, 31–39.

Donachy, W. (1979) 'Parental participation in pre-school education'. In Clark, M. M. and Cheyne, W. M. (eds) *Studies in Pre-school Education*. Sevenoaks: Hodder & Stoughton.

Donachy, W. (1987) 'Parental participation in a language programme'. In Clark, M. M. (ed.) *Roles, Responsibilities and Relationships in the Education of the Young Child*, Educational Review Occasional Publication No. 13. University of Birmingham.

Donaldson, M. (1978) *Children's Minds*. London: Fontana.

Dunn, L., Dunn, L. and Whetton, C. (1982) *British Picture Vocabulary Scale*. Windsor: NFER-Nelson.

Dunn, L. M., Horton, K. B. and Smith, J. O. (1968) *Peabody Language Development Kits*. Minnesota: American Guidance Service.

Dunn, S. and Morgan, V. (1987) 'Nursery and infant school play patterns: sex-related differences'. *British Educational Research Journal*, **13**, pp. 271–281.

Dye, J. S. (1984) 'Early education matters: a study of pre-school curriculum content'. *Educational Research*, **26**, pp. 95–105.

Ellender, P. (1983) 'A formative evaluation of a voluntary Portage Group'. *Occasional Papers of the Division of Educational and Child Psychology of the BPS*, **7**, p. 77–78.

Elliot, C. D., Murray, J. D. and Pearson, L. S. (1983) *British Ability Scales – Revised*. Windsor: NFER-Nelson.

Ervin-Tripp, S. and Mitchell-Kernan, C. (1977) *Child Discourse*. New York: Academic Press.

Evans, M. and Wright, A. (1987) 'A task analysis of setting up a Portage scheme'. In Hedderley, R. and Jennings, K. (eds) *Extending Portage*. Windsor: NFER-Nelson.

Fagot, B. I. (1973) 'Influence of teacher behaviour in the preschool'. *Developmental Psychology*, **9**, pp. 198–206.

Ferri, E., Birchall, D., Gingell, V. and Gipps, C. (1981) *Combined Nursery*

Centres. London: National Children's Bureau.

Finch, J. (1984) 'A first-class environment? Working class playgroups as pre-school experience'. *British Educational Research Journal*, **10**, pp. 3–17.

Fish, J. (1985) *Special Education: The Way Ahead*. Milton Keynes: Open University Press.

Flowers, C. (1988) 'Creche course in success'. *Scotsman*, 3 May.

Frederickson, N. and Haran, H. (1986) 'Portage evaluation and re-evaluation: a day nursery project'. *Educational Psychology in Practice*, **1**, pp. 159–165.

Gahagan, D. M. and Gahagan, G. A. (1970) *Talk Reform*. London: Routledge & Kegan Paul.

Garland, C. and White, S. (1980) *Children and Day Nurseries*. London: Grant McIntyre.

Garvey, C. (1983) 'Some properties of social play'. In Donaldson, M., Grieve, R. and Pratt, C. (eds) *Early Childhood Development and Education*. Oxford: Blackwell.

Gipps, C. (1982a) 'Nursery nurses and nursery teachers I: their assessment of children's verbal-social behaviour'. *Journal of Child Psychology and Psychiatry*, **23**, pp. 237–254.

Gipps, C. (1982b) 'Nursery nurses and nursery teachers II: their attitudes towards pre-school children and their parents'. *Journal of Child Psychology and Psychiatry*, **23**, pp. 255–265.

Goffman, I. (1976) *Frames of Mind*. Harmondsworth: Penguin.

Goldstein, H, and Wickstrom, S. (1986) 'Peer intervention effects on communicative interaction among handicapped and non-handicapped preschoolers'. *Journal of Applied Behaviour Analysis*, **19**, pp. 209–214.

Gosling, J. (1981) 'Kinesics in discourse'. In Coulthard, M. and Montgomery, M. (eds) *Studies in Discourse Analysis*. London: Routledge & Kegan Paul.

Greenwood, C. R., Dinwiddie, G., Bailey, V. *et al.* (1987) 'Field replication of classwide peer tutoring'. *Journal of Applied Behaviour Analysis*, **20**, pp. 151–160.

Grunwell, P. (1985) *Phonological Assessment of Child Speech (PACS)*. Windsor: NFER-Nelson.

Grunwell, P. (1987) *PACS Pictures: Language Elicitation Materials*. Windsor: NFER-Nelson.

Gulliford, R. (1971) *Special Educational Needs*. London: Routledge & Kegan Paul.

Gulliford, R. (1983) 'The school's role in assessment'. *Special Education – Forward Trends*, **10**, pp. 6–9.

Gunstone, C., Hogg, J., Sebba, J., Warner, J. and Almond, S. (1982) *Classroom Provision and Organisation for Integrated Pre-School Provision, Anson House Preschool Project Paper 2*. Barkingside: Barnardo's.

Guralnick, M. J. (1976) 'The value of integrating handicapped and non-handicapped preschool children'. *American Journal of Orthopsychiatry*, **46**, pp. 236–245.

Gutfreund, M. (1988) *Bristol Language Development Scales*. Windsor: NFER-Nelson.

Hackett, G. (1987) 'Burnt out in the academic nursery'. *Times Educational Supplement*, 18 September.

Hagedorn, J. (1986) 'Plan to end "chaos" in under-5 training'. *Times Educational Supplement*, 5 December.

Halloran, H. (1982) *The Diverse Role of the Nursery Nurse in Its Implications for Future Education and Training*, Unpublished M. Ed. thesis, University of Manchester.

Hamilton, V. J. and Gordon, D. A. (1978) 'Teacher–child interactions in preschool and task persistence'. *American Educational Research Journal*, **15**, pp. 459–466.

Hartley, R. E. (1971) 'Play, the essential ingredient'. *Childhood Education*, **48**, pp. 80–84.

Heaslip, P. (1985) 'The training and roles of nursery staff (research summary)'. *Tutors of Advanced Courses for Teachers of Young Children*, **5**, no. 2.

Heaslip, P. (1987) 'Does the glass slipper fit Cinderella? Nursery teachers and their training'. In Clark, M. M. (ed.) *Roles, Responsibilities and Relationships in the Education of the Young Child*, Educational Review Occasional Publication No. 13. University of Birmingham.

Hedderley, R. and Jennings, K. (1987) *Extending Portage*. Windsor: NFER-Nelson.

Hegarty, S. (1987) *Meeting Special Needs in Ordinary Schools*. London: Cassell.

Hegarty, S. and Pocklington, K. (1981) *Educating Pupils with Special Needs in the Ordinary School*. Windsor: NFER-Nelson.

Hellier, C. (1988) 'Research in practice'. *Scottish Association of Local Government and Educational Psychologists Quarterly*, **7**, pp. 4–7.

Henderson, D. (1987) 'Strathclyde plans to axe nurseries'. *Times Educational Supplement (Scotland)*, August.

Hirst, P. H. (1969) 'The logic of curriculum'. *Journal of Curriculum Studies*, **1**, pp. 142–158.

Holmes, A. and McMahon, L. (1978) *Learning from Observation: a Guide to Using 'Observing Children' in Playgroup Training and Support*. Oxford Pre-School Research Group.

Hopkins, D. (1984a) 'Teacher research: back to basics'. *Classroom Action Research Network Bulletin*, **6**, pp. 94–99.

Hopkins, D. (1984b) 'Towards a methodology for teacher based classroom research'. *School Organisation*, **4**, pp. 197–204.

Hopkins, D. (1985) *A Teacher's Guide to Classroom Research*. Milton Keynes: Open University Press.

Horne, B. M. and Philleo, L. L. (1976) 'A comparative study of the spontaneous play activities of normal and mentally defective children'. In Bruner, J. S., Jolly, A. and Sylva, K. (eds) *Play: Its Role in Development and Evolution*. New York: Basic Books.

Hughes, M. (1975) *Egocentrism in Pre-School Children*, unpublished doctoral dissertation, Edinburgh University.

Hughes, M., Carmichael, H., Pinkerton, G. and Tizard, B. (1979) 'Recording children's conversations at home and at nursery school: a technique and some methodological considerations'. *Journal of Child Psychology and Psychiatry*, **20**, pp. 225–232.

Hughes, M., Mayall, B., Moss, P., Perry, J., Petrie, P. and Pinkerton, G. (1980) *Nurseries Now*. Harmondsworth: Penguin.
Huntley, M. (1985) *Reynell Developmental Language Scales: Second Revision*. Windsor: NFER-Nelson.
Hutt, C. (1970) 'Specific and diverse exploration'. In Reese, H. W. and Lipsitt, L. P. (eds) *Advances in Child Development and Behaviour*, **5**, pp. 119–180.
Hutt, C. and Vaizey, M. J. (1966) 'Differential effects of group density on social behaviour'. *Nature*, **209**, pp. 1371–1372.

Ingram, T. T. S. (1965) 'Specific retardation of speech development'. *Speech Pathology Therapy*, **8**, pp. 3–11.

James, S. D. and Egel, A. L. (1986) 'A direct prompting strategy for increasing reciprocal interactions between handicapped and non-handicapped siblings'. *Journal of Applied Behaviour Analysis*, **19**, pp. 173–186.
Jeffree, D. and McConkey, R. (1976) *Let Me Speak*. London: Souvenir Press.
Jeffree, D. M., McConkey, R. and Hewson, S. (1977) *Let Me Play*. London: Souvenir Press.
Johnson, S. M. and Bolstad, O. D. (1975) 'Reactivity to home observation: a comparison of audio recorded behaviour with observers present or absent'. *Journal of Applied Behaviour Analysis*, **8**, pp. 181–185.
Jowett, S. and Sylva, K. (1986) 'Does kind of pre-school matter?' *Educational Research*, **28**, pp. 21–31.

Kanner, L. (1957) *Child Psychiatry*. Illinois: Springer.
Kaplan-Sanoff, M. A. (1978) 'Mainstreaming: an evaluation of the integrated preschool'. *Dissertation Abstracts International*, **39**, p. 758-A.
Katz, L. G. (1985) 'Fostering communicative competence in young children'. In Clark, M. M. (ed.) *Helping Communication in Early Education*, Educational Review Occasional Publication No. 11. University of Birmingham.
Kiernan, C. and Jones, M. (1982) *Behaviour Assessment Battery*. Windsor: NFER-Nelson.
Kent, J. and Kent, P. (1970) *Nursery Schools for All*. London: Ward Lock Educational.
Kirby, F. D. and Toler, H. C. (1970) 'Modification of preschool isolate behaviour – a case study'. *Journal of Applied Behaviour Analysis*, **3**, pp. 309–314.
Kohlberg, L. (1972) 'Early education: a cognitive – developmental view'. In Lavatelli, C. S. and Stendler, F. (eds) *Readings in Child Behaviour and Development*. New York: Harcourt Brace Jovanovich.

Labov, W. (1972) *Sociolinguistic Patterns*. Philadelphia: University of Pennsylvania Press.
Laing, A. (1979) 'School-based programmes'. In Laing, A. (ed.) *Young Children with Special Needs*. University College of Swansea.
Land, A. (1985) 'Portage – parents' views'. *Educational Psychology in Practice*, **1**, pp. 120–123.

Lazar, I. (1978) *Lasting Effects of Pre-School: a report of the Consortium for Longitudinal Studies Education Commission of the States*, Denver, Colorado.

Leiter, R. (1948) *Leiter International Performance Scale Battery for Children.* Windsor: NFER-Nelson.

Light, P. (1979) *The Development of Social Sensitivity.* Cambridge: Cambridge University Press.

Lilley, I. M. (1967) *Froebel: a Selection from his Writings.* Cambridge: Cambridge University Press.

Lindsay, G. and Dale, P. (1982) 'The integration of children with special educational needs into nursery schools'. *Occasional Papers of the Division of Educational and Child Psychology*, **6**, pp. 42–49.

Lindsay, G. and Desforges, M. (1986) 'Integrated nurseries for children with special educational needs'. *British Journal of Special Education*, **13**, pp. 63–66.

Lister, T. (1985) 'Portage – eight years on'. In Daly, B., Addington, J., Kerfoot, S. and Sigston, M. (eds) *Portage: the Importance of Parents.* Windsor: NFER-Nelson.

Livingston, J. (1987) 'Robbing Peter to pay Paul'. *Times Educational Supplement (Scotland)*, 18 September.

Lloyd, I. (1983) 'The aims of early childhood education'. In Clark, M. M. and Wade, B. (eds) *Early Childhood Education, Educational Review Special Issue 15*, **35**, pp. 113–120.

Lomax, C. (1977) 'Record keeping in nursery school'. *Educational Research*, **19**, no. 3, 192–198.

Lomax, C. (1979) 'Psychological research and early education'. In Clark, M. M. and Cheyne, W. M. (eds) *Studies in Pre-School Education.* Sevenoaks: Hodder & Stoughton.

Loo, C. M. (1972) 'The effects of spatial density on the social behaviour of children'. *Journal of Applied Social Psychology*, **2**, pp. 372–381.

Lorenz, S. (1987) 'The Salford Portage in Nurseries Project (SPIN)'. In Hedderley, R. and Jennings, K. (eds) *Extending Portage.* Windsor: NFER-Nelson.

Lovell, K., Hoyle, H. W. and Siddall, M. C. (1968) 'A study of some aspects of the play and language of young children in delayed speech'. *Journal of Child Psychology and Psychiatry*, **9**, pp. 41–50.

Ludlow, J. R. and Allen, L. M. (1979) 'The effect of early intervention and pre-school stimulus on the development of the Down's Syndrome child'. *Journal of Mental Deficiency Research*, **23**, pp. 29–44.

McBrien, T. and Foxen, T. (1981) *Training Staff in Behavioural Methods Instructor's Handbook and Trainee Workbook.* Manchester: Manchester University Press.

McConkey, R. (1980) *Learning to Pretend: a Handbook for Staff and Parents.* Dublin: St Michael's House.

McConkey, R. (1983) 'New approaches to parental involvement in pre-school education'. In Clark, M. M. (ed.) *Special Educational Needs and Children Under Five*, Educational Review Occasional Publication No. 9. University of Birmingham.

McConkey, R. (1985) 'Play: a review of research in the field of mental handicap'. In Lane, D. and Stratford, B. (eds) *Current Approaches to Down's Syndrome*. Eastbourne: Holt-Saunders.

McConkey, R. (1986) 'Changing beliefs about play and handicapped children'. In Smith, P. K. (ed.) *Children's Play: Research Developments and Practical Applications*. London: Gordon and Breach.

McConkey, R., Jeffree, D. and Hewson, S. (1979) 'Involving parents in extending the language development of their young mentally handicapped children'. *British Journal of Disorders of Communication*, **14**, pp. 13–17.

MacDonald, A. M. (1972) *Chambers Twentieth Century Dictionary*. Edinburgh: W & R Chambers.

McGrew, P. L. (1970) 'Social and spatial density effects on spacing behaviour in preschool children'. *Journal of Child Psychology and Psychiatry*, **11**, pp. 197–205.

McGrew, W. C. (1972a) *An Ethological Study of Children's Behaviour*. London: Academic Press.

McGrew, W. C. (1972b) 'Aspects of social development in nursery school children with emphasis on introduction to the group'. In Blurton-Jones, N. (ed.) *Ethological Studies of Child Behaviour*. Cambridge: Cambridge University Press.

Mcguire, J. and Richman, N. (1987) *The Pre-School Behaviour Checklist*. Windsor: NFER-Nelson.

MacLure, M. and French, P. (1981) 'A comparison of talk at home and at school'. In Wells, G. (ed.) *Learning Through Interaction: the Study of Language Development*. Cambridge: Cambridge University Press.

McNally, D. W. (1981) 'Preoperational thought'. In Roberts, M. and Tamburrini, J. (eds) *Child Development 0–5*. Edinburgh: Holmes McDougall.

McQuaid, C. (1986) 'Ulster ponders handicap attitude'. *Times Educational Supplement*, 7 November.

McTear, M. (1985) *Children's Conversation*. Oxford: Blackwell.

Makins, V. (1981) 'Day nurseries damage children'. *Times Educational Supplement*, 24 July.

Manning, K. and Sharp, A. (1977) *Structuring Play in the Early Years at School*. London: Ward Lock.

Merrett, F. E. (1981) 'Studies in behaviour modification in British educational settings'. *Educational Psychology*, (v), **1**, pp. 13–38.

Millward, V. (1988) 'Cut-price professionals?' *Times Educational Supplement (Scotland)*, January.

Mittler, P. (1970) 'Language disorders'. In Mittler, P. (ed.) *The Psychological Assessment of Mental and Physical Handicaps*. London: Methuen.

Mittler, P. (1983) 'Planning for future developments'. In Mittler, P. and McConachie, H. (eds) *Parents, Professionals and Mentally Handicapped People: Approaches to Partnership*. Beckenham: Croom Helm.

Mittler, P. (1987) '"Parents are welcome in my school at any time": rhetoric or reality?' In Cross, D. (ed.) *Models of Co-operation in Special Education*, Proceedings of the 10th National Conference of the Australian Association of Special Education, Launceston, Tasmania.

Mogford, K. (1977) 'The play of handicapped children'. In Tizard, B. and Harvey, D. (eds) *Biology of Play*. Philadelphia: Lippincott.

Moore, E. and Sylva, K. (1984) 'A survey of under-fives record-keeping in Great Britain'. *Educational Research*, **26**, pp. 115–120.

Morgenstern, M., Low-Beer, H. and Morgenstern, F. (1966) *Practical Training for the Severely Handicapped Child*. London: Heinemann.

Mortimer, H. (1986) 'Special preparations'. *Child Education*, June, pp. 10–11.

Muller, D. J., Munro, S. M. and Code, C. (1981) *Language Assessment for Remediation*. London: Croom Helm.

Newman, V. and Pitchford, M. (1988) 'Modifying aggressive behaviour: a case study of a four year old in a nursery school'. *Educational Psychology in Practice*, **3**, pp. 29–34.

Nixon, J. (1981) *A Teacher's Guide to Action Research: Evaluation, Enquiry and Development in the Classroom*. London:Grant McIntyre.

Northam, J. (1983) 'The myth of the pre-school'. *Education*, **11**, pp. 37–40.

Odom, S. L., Hoyson, M., Jamieson, B. and Strain, P. S. (1985) 'Increasing handicapped preschoolers' peer social interactions: cross setting and component analysis'. *Journal of Applied Behaviour Analysis*, **18**, pp. 3–16.

Parten, M. B. (1932) 'Social participation among pre-school children'. *Journal of Abnormal and Social Psychology*, **27**, pp. 243–269.

Passmore, B. (1980) 'Nursery law to be changed – statutory duty will go'. *Times Educational Supplement*, 8 February.

Payne, G. (1985) 'Planning activities that will provide appropriate contexts to promote adult–child and child–child communication in the nursery unit'. In Clark, M. M. (ed.) *Helping Communication in Early Education*, Educational Review Occasional Publication No. 11. University of Birmingham.

Penn, H. (1987) 'Why the nursery sector is crying out for reform'. *Times Educational Supplement (Scotland)*, 11 September.

Peterson, N. L. and Haralick, J. G. (1977) 'Integration of handicapped and non-handicapped preschoolers – an analysis of play behaviour and social integration'. *Education and Training of the Mentally Retarded*, **12**, pp. 235–245.

Piaget, J. (1963) *Psychology of Intelligence*. New Jersey: Littlefield, Adams.

Piaget, J. and Inhelder, B. (1956) *The Child's Conception of Space*. London: Routledge & Kegan Paul.

Plowden, Lady (1982) 'Presidential address to the Pre-school Playgroups Association'. *Times Educational Supplement*, 2 April.

Pugh, G. (1981a) 'Parent workshops: an overview'. In Pugh, G. (ed.) *Parents as Partners*. London: National Children's Bureau.

Pugh, G. (1981b) 'Honeylands Home Visiting Project, Exeter'. In Pugh, G. (ed.) *Parents as Partners*. London: National Children's Bureau.

Pugh, G. and Russell, P. (1977) *Shared Care: Support Services for Families with Handicapped Children*. London: National Children's Bureau.

Quinn, J. M. and Rubin, K. H. (1984) 'The play of handicapped children'. In Yawkey, T. D. and Pellegrini, A. D. (eds) *Child's Play: Developmental and Applied*. New York: Lawrence Erlbaum Association.

Rathbone, M. and Wheldall, K. (1976) 'Mother knows, too'. *Contact*, July.
Raven, J. (1980) *Parents, Teachers and Children*. Edinburgh: SCRE.
Reynell, J. and Zinkin, P. (1979) *Reynell–Zinkin Scales for Young Visually Handicapped Children*. Windsor: NFER-Nelson.
Rheubottom, S. (1983) 'Handicapped child = taxi'. In Mittler, P. and McConachie, H. (eds) *Parents, Professionals and Mentally Handicapped People: Approaches to Partnership*. Beckenham: Croom Helm.
Robson, B. (1983) 'Encouraging dialogue in pre-school units: the role of the Pink Pamfer'. In Clark, M. M. and Wade, B. (eds) *Early Childhood Education*, Educational Review Special Issue No. 15. University of Birmingham.
Robson, B. (1985) *Young Children with Special Educational Needs – Integration and Segregation*, unpublished doctoral thesis, University of Birmingham.
Robson, C. (1979) *Language Development through Structured Teaching: a Mini Course for Teachers of the Mentally Handicapped*. Huddersfield Polytechnic.
Romaine, S. (1984) *The Language of Children and Adolescents: the Acquisition of Communicative Competence*. Oxford: Blackwell.
Rustin, L. (1987) *Assessment and Therapy Programme for Dysfluent Children*. Windsor: NFER-Nelson.
Rutherford, B. (1986) 'Two and a half years of recording – a schizophrenic response'. In Wilkinson, J. (ed.) *Warnock Seven Years On: a Scottish Perspective*. Glasgow: National Children's Bureau.

Sainato, D. M., Maheady, L. and Shook, G. L. (1986) 'The effects of a classroom manager role on the social interaction patterns and social status of withdrawn kindergarten children'. *Journal of Applied Behaviour Analysis*, **9**, pp. 187–195.
Sandler, A. M. and Wills, D. M. (1965) 'Preliminary notes on play in the blind child'. *Journal of Child Psychotherapy*, **1**, pp. 7–10.
Sasso, G. M. and Rude, H. A. (1987) 'Unprogrammed effects of training high-status peers to interact with severely handicapped children'. *Journal of Applied Behaviour Analysis*, **20**, pp. 35–44.
Savage, F. (1987) 'Psychologists and research'. *Scottish Association of Local Government Educational Psychologists*, **6**, pp. 12–14.
Scottish Education Department (1971) *Before Five*. Edinburgh: HMSO.
Scottish Education Department (1983a) *Identification, Assessment and Recording*, (Circular, 10/83).
Scottish Education Department (1983b) *Special Educational Needs: a Guide for Parents*. Edinburgh: HMSO.
Sebba, J. (1980) *A System for Assessment and Intervention for Preschool Profoundly Retarded Multiply Handicapped Children*. Barkingside: Barnardo's.
Sebba, J. (1981) 'Social interactions among pre-school handicapped and non-handicapped children'. Paper presented at British Psychological Society Annual Conference.
Sewell, L. (1986) 'In my view'. *Child Education*, August, p. 13.
Sharp, C. (1988) 'Starting school at four'. *Research Papers in Education*, **3**, pp. 64–90.

Sigel, I. E. (1969) 'The Piagetian system and the world of education'. In Elkind, D. and Flavell, J. H. (eds) *Studies in Cognitive Development*. Oxford: Oxford University Press.

Sinson, J. C. and Wetherick, N. E. (1981) 'The behaviour of children with Down Syndrome in normal playgroups'. *Journal of Mental Deficiency Research*, **25**, pp. 113–120.

Smilansky, S. (1968) *The Effects of Sociodramatic Play on Disadvantaged Preschool Children*. New York: Wiley.

Smith, L. (1985) 'Making sense of Piaget's psychology'. *Oxford Review of Education*, **11**, pp. 181–191.

Smith, P. (1976) 'Social and fantasy play in young children'. In Tizard, B. and Harvey, D. (eds) *Play in Childhood*. London: Heinemann Medical Books & Spastics International Medical Publications.

Smith, P. K. (1978) 'A longitudinal study of social participation in preschool children – solitary and parallel play re-examined'. *Developmental Psychology*, **14**, pp. 517–523.

Smith, P. K. and Connolly, K. J. (1980) *The Ecology of Pre-School Behaviour*. Cambridge: Cambridge University Press.

Smith, P. K. and Syddall, S. (1978) 'Play and non-play tutoring in pre-school children: is it play or tutoring which matters?' *British Journal of Educational Psychology*, **48**, pp. 315–325.

Smith, T. (1980) *Parents and Pre-School*. London: Grant McIntyre.

Snijders, J. and Snijders-Oomen, N. (1976) *Snijders-Oomen Non-Verbal Intelligence Scale*. Windsor: NFER-Nelson.

Strain, P. S. and Shores, R. E. (1977) 'Social interaction development among behaviourally handicapped pre-school children'. *Psychology in the Schools*, **14**, pp. 493–502.

Strain, P. S., Shores, R. E. and Kerr, M. M. (1976) 'An experimental analysis of "spillover" effects on the social interaction of behaviourally handicapped preschool children'. *Journal of Applied Behaviour Analysis*, **9**, pp. 31–40.

Strain, P. S., Shores, R. E. and Timm, M. A. (1977) 'Effects of peer social initiations on the behaviour of withdrawn preschool children'. *Journal of Applied Behaviour Analysis*, **10**, pp. 289–298.

Strathclyde Regional Council (1985) *Under Fives: Final Report of the Member/Officer Group*. Glasgow: Strathclyde Regional Council.

Stubbs, M. (1981) 'Scratching the surface: linguistic data in educational research'. In Adelman, C. (ed.) *Uttering, Muttering*. London: Grant-McIntyre.

Stubbs, M. (1983) *Discourse Analysis: the Sociolinguistic Analysis of Natural Language*. Oxford: Blackwell.

Stutsman, R. (1931) *Merrill–Palmer Pre-School Performance Scale*. Windsor: NFER-Nelson.

Sutton-Smith, B. and Kelly-Byrne, D. (1984) 'The phenomenon of bipolarity in play theories'. In Yawkey, T. D. and Pellegrini, A. D. (eds) *Child's Play: Developmental and Applied*. New Jersey: Lawrence Erlbaum Association.

Swann, W. (1985) 'Is the integration of children with special needs happening?: an analysis of recent statistics of pupils in special schools'. *Oxford Review of Education*, **11**, pp. 3–18.

Sylva, K., Bruner, J. S. and Geneva, P. (1976) 'The role of play in the problem solving of children 3–5 years old'. In Bruner, J. S., Jolly, A. and Sylva, K. (eds) *Play: Its Role in Development and Evolution*. New York: Basic Books.

Sylva, K., Painter, M. and Roy, C. (1979) *Observing Children*. Oxford Pre-School Research Group.

Sylva, K., Roy, C. and Painter, M. (1980) *Childwatching at Playgroup and Nursery School*. London: Grant McIntyre.

Tait. P. (1972) 'Behaviour of young blind children in a controlled play session'. *Perception and Motor Skills*, **34**, pp. 963–969.

Taylor, P. (1970) *Curriculum Planning for Compensatory Education: a Suggested Procedure*. London: Schools Council.

Taylor, P. H., Exon, G. and Holley, B. (1972) *A Study of Nursery Education*, Schools Council Working Paper 41. London: Evans/Methuen Educational.

Taylor, W. (1980) 'Professional or personal development?' In Hoyle, E. and Megarry, J. (eds) *Professional Development of Teachers – World Yearbook of Education*. London: Kogan Page and Nichols.

Terman, L. M. and Merrill, M. A. (1960) *Stanford–Binet Intelligence Scale (Form L–M)*. London: George Harrap & Co.

Thomson, G., Budge, A., Buultjens, M. and Lee, M. (1986) 'Scotland and the 1981 Education Act'. *British Journal of Special Education*, **13**, pp. 115–118.

Thorndike, R. L. (1973) *Stanford–Binet Intelligence Scale 1972 Norms Tables*. Boston: Houghton Mifflin Co.

Threlfall, S. (1979) 'The counselling of parents'. In Laing, A. F. (ed.) *Young Children with Special Needs*. University College of Swansea.

Tizard, B. (1975) *Early Childhood Education*. Slough: NFER.

Tizard, B. (1976) 'Play: the child's way of learning?' In Tizard, B. and Harvey, D. (eds) *Play in Childhood*, Clinics in Development Medicine. London: Spastics International Publications.

Tizard, B. (1986) *The Care of Young Children: the Implications of Recent Research*. London: Thomas Coram Research Unit.

Tizard, B. and Hughes, M. (1984) *Young Children Learning*. London: Fontana.

Tizard, B., Mortimore, J. and Burchell, B. (1981) *Involving Parents in Nursery and Infant Schools*. London: Grant McIntyre.

Tizard, B., Philps, J. and Plewis, I. (1976a) 'Staff behaviour in pre-school centres'. *Journal of Child Psychology and Psychiatry*, **17**, pp. 21–33.

Tizard, B., Philps, J. and Plewis, I. (1976b) 'Play in pre-school centres – I. Play measures and their relation to age, sex and IQ'. *Journal of Child Psychology and Psychiatry*, **17**, pp. 251–264.

Tizard, B., Philps, J. and Plewis, I. (1976c) 'Play in pre-school centres – II. Effects on play of the child's social class and of the educational orientation of the centre'. *Journal of Child Psychology and Psychiatry*, **17**, pp. 265–274.

Tizard, J. (1975) 'The objectives and organisation of educational and day care services for young children'. *Oxford Review of Education*, **3**, pp. 211–221.

Todd, R. (1981) 'Methodology: the hidden context of situation in studies of talk'. In Adelman, C. (ed.) *Uttering, Muttering*. London: Grant McIntyre.

Tough, J. (1973a) *Focus on Meaning*. London: George Allen and Unwin.

Tough, J. (1973b) 'The language of young children: the implications for the education of the young disadvantaged child'. In Chazan, M. (ed.) *Education in the Early Years*. University College of Swansea.

Tough, J. (1977) *Talking and Learning*. London: Ward Lock Educational.

Twistleton, M. (1980) *An Evaluation of the Referral Process to Nursery Facilities for Children with Special Educational Needs*, unpublished MSc special study, Division of Education, Sheffield University.

Tyler, S. (1980) *Keele Pre-School Assessment Guide*. Windsor: NFER-Nelson.

Umiker-Sebeok, D. J. (1979) Pre-school children's intraconversational narratives. *Journal of Child Language*, **6**, pp. 91–109.

van der Eyken, W. (1977) *The Pre-School Years*. Harmondsworth: Penguin.

Warnock, N. J. (1976) 'Making general education "special"'. *Education and Training of the Mentally Retarded*, **11**, pp. 304–307.

Watson, T. J. (1973) 'Integration of hearing impaired children in nursery schools in England'. In Northcott, W. H. (ed.) *The Hearing Impaired Child in the Regular Classroom – Preschool, Elementary and Secondary Years*. Washington: Alexander Graham Bell Association for the Deaf.

Watt, J. (1977) *Co-operation in Pre-School Education*. London: SSRC.

Watt, J. (1983) 'In-service education: an opportunity for growth?' *Educational Review*, **35**, pp. 195–201.

Watt, J. (1987) 'Continuity in early education'. In Clark, M. M. (ed.) *Roles, Responsibilities and Relationships in the Education of the Young Child*, Educational Review Occasional Publications No. 13. University of Birmingham.

Watt, J. and Flett, M. (1985) *Continuity in Early Education: the Role of Parents*. Mimeo, Department of Education, Aberdeen University.

Webb, L. (1974) *Purpose and Practice in Nursery Education*. Oxford: Blackwell.

Webster, A. and Ellwood, J. (1985) *The Hearing-Impaired Child in the Ordinary School*. Beckenham: Croom Helm.

Webster, A. and McConnell, C. (1987) *Children with Speech and Language Difficulties*. London: Cassell.

Weikart, D., Epstein, A., Schweinhart, L. and Bond, J. (1978) *The Ypsilanti Pre-school Curriculum Demonstration Project: Pre-school Years and Longitudinal Results*. Monographs of the High/Scope Ed. Research Foundation, No. 4.

Weiss, R. (1981) 'INREAL intervention for language handicapped and bilingual children'. *Journal of the Division for Early Childhood*, **4**, pp. 24–27.

Wells, G. (1981) *Learning Through Interaction*. Cambridge: Cambridge University Press.

Wells, G. (1985) *Language Development in the Pre-School Years*. Cambridge: Cambridge University Press.

Weschler, D. (1967) *Manual for the Weschler Preschool and Primary Scale of Intelligence*. New York: Psychological Corporation.

Wheldall, K. (1987) *Sentence Comprehension Test – Revised*. Windsor: NFER-Nelson.

Wheldall, K., Mittler, P. and Hobsbaum, A. (1979) *Sentence Comprehension Test*. Windsor: NFER-Nelson.

Wheldall, K. and Wheldall, D. (1980) 'School meals, praise and contingent dessert: an attempt to improve eating behaviour in the nursery class.' Paper read at Conference of the Association for Behaviour Modification with Children at Coventry.

Widerstrom, A. H. (1983) 'How important is play for handicapped children?' *Childhood Education*, **60**, pp. 39–50.

Widerstrom, A. H. (1986) 'Educating young handicapped children – what can early childhood education contribute?' *Childhood Education*, December, pp. 78–83.

Wiehl, P. and Barrow, P. (1987) 'Portage in Bradford: training volunteers'. In Hedderley, R. and Jennings, K. (eds) *Extending Portage*. Windsor: NFER-Nelson.

Wilce, H. (1987) 'Cashing in on childhood'. *Times Educational Supplement*, 9 October.

Wilcock, P. (1981) 'The Portage Project in America', In Pugh, G. (ed.) *Parents as Partners*. London: National Children's Bureau.

Willes, M. (1981) 'Children becoming pupils: a study of discourse in nursery and reception classes'. In Adelman, C. (ed.) *Uttering, Muttering*. London: Grant McIntyre.

Winnicott, D. W. (1964) *The Child, The Family and the Outside World*. Harmondsworth: Penguin.

Wintre, M. G. and Webster, C. D. (1974) 'A brief report on using a traditional social behaviour scale with disturbed children'. *Journal of Applied Behaviour Analysis*, **7**, pp. 345–348.

Wolfendale, S. (1987) *Primary Schools and Special Needs: Policy, Planning and Provision*. London: Cassell.

Wood, D., McMahon, L. and Cranstoun, Y. (1980) *Working with Under Fives*. London: Grant McIntyre.

Wood, H. A. and Wood, D. J. (1983) 'Questioning the pre-school child'. *Educational Review*, **35**, pp. 149–162.

Wood, H. A. and Wood, D. J. (1984) 'An experimental evaluation of the effects of five styles of teacher conversation on the language of hearing-impaired children'. *Journal of Child Psychology and Psychiatry*, **25**, pp. 45–62.

Woodhead, M. (1979) *Pre-school Education in Western Europe: Issues, Policies and Trends*. London: Longman.

Name Index

Subject Index